THE CHARTERS OF FREEDOM

"A NEW WORLD IS AT HAND"

THE CHARTERS OF FREEDOM

"A New World Is at Hand"

BASED ON AN EXHIBITION IN THE NATIONAL ARCHIVES
ROTUNDA FOR THE CHARTERS OF FREEDOM

Stacey Bredhoff

With a Foreword by John W. Carlin,
Eighth Archivist of the United States

The Foundation for the National Archives, Washington, DC
in association with D Giles Limited, London

page 2
Bronze medallion inlay on the floor of the
National Archives Rotunda

page 7
Detail, bronze inlay design on the floor of the
National Archives Rotunda

page 8
Detail, bronze gate in the National Archives
Rotunda

Table of Contents

"A New World Is at Hand"
Stacey Bredhoff

THE EXHIBITION, "A NEW WORLD IS AT HAND,"
OPENED IN THE ROTUNDA
OF THE NATIONAL ARCHIVES BUILDING
ON SEPTEMBER 17, 2003.
THE DOCUMENTS FLANKING THE
PERMANENT DISPLAY OF THE
DECLARATION OF INDEPENDENCE, CONSTITUTION, AND BILL OF
RIGHTS ARE CHANGED PERIODICALLY IN THE INTEREST OF THEIR
LONG-TERM PRESERVATION.

The Charters of Freedom—the Declaration of Independence, Constitution, and Bill of Rights—were installed in the National Archives Rotunda in December 1952. President Harry S. Truman presided over the dedication ceremony held there on December 15, the 161st anniversary of the ratification of the Bill of Rights.

A half century later, following a major renovation of the National Archives Building and the re-encasement of the Charters of Freedom, President George W. Bush presided over the rededication of the Rotunda. That ceremony took place on September 17, 2003, the 216th anniversary of the signing of the Constitution.

The Constitution and the Declaration can live only as long as they are enshrined in our hearts and minds. If they are not so enshrined, they would be no better than mummies in their glass cases and they could in time become idols whose worship would be a grim mockery of the true faith. Only as these documents are reflected in the thought and acts of Americans can they remain symbols of power that can move the world. . . .

So I confidently predict that what we are doing today is placing before the eyes of many generations to come the symbols of a living faith. And, like the sight of the flag "in the dawn's early light," the sight of these symbols will lift up their hearts, so they will go out of this building helped and strengthened and inspired.

The courage of America's first leaders gave us the Declaration. Their patience and wisdom gave us the Constitution. They were patient through long and contentious and learned debates and discussions. They were wise in their understanding of human nature, with all its virtues and all the temptations. The supreme law of this land is the work of practical minds addressed to practical questions . . .

. . . The American people can take pride in the care we have given to preserving the work of the founding generation. Their words first guided a nation of scarcely 4 million souls. Yet even in their own day, the founders knew they had put large events in motion, and free people everywhere remain in their debt.

In this rotunda are the most cherished material possessions of a great and good nation. By this rededication, we show our deep respect for the first principles of our republic, and our lasting gratitude to those first citizens of the United States of America.

Gracing the curved walls of the Rotunda are two murals painted by artist Barry Faulkner in 1935–36. They were created to animate the grand architecture of the Rotunda and to convey to visitors the importance of the Charters documents. On the left wall, *The Declaration of Independence* (above) shows Thomas Jefferson presenting a draft of the Declaration to John Hancock, President of the Continental Congress. On the right wall, *The Constitution of the United States* (following spread) shows James Madison offering the final draft of the Constitution to George Washington, President of the Constitutional Convention.

Measuring 14' x 35', they are among the largest single-piece oil-on-canvas murals in the United States. To accommodate their enormous size, these murals were painted in a specially designed studio above Grand Central Station in New York City, subsequently rolled onto custom-made drums, and shipped to Washington, DC, where they were affixed to the Rotunda walls.

THE UNITED STATES 1789

FOREWORD
By John W. Carlin, Eighth Archivist of the United States

The National Archives Rotunda is the permanent home of the Declaration of Independence, Constitution, and Bill of Rights. There, these great documents, known collectively as the Charters of Freedom, are on public view 364 days a year—every day except December 25. Millions of people from around the world have seen them there since they were installed in 1952.

"A New World Is at Hand," the exhibition flanking the permanent display of the Charters, presents glimpses of the breathtaking story of how the Charters were created and the impact they have had on the course of history in the United States and around the world. Highlights of that dramatic story, chronicled by a selection of milestone documents from the National Archives holdings, are presented in this book.

Beginning with the 1775 Proclamation of King George III labeling the colonists as "traitors," the story of the American Revolution takes life; the courage of the Founders, their passion for liberty, their political genius are all revealed in the pages that tell their story. The landmark Supreme Court case, *Marbury* v. *Madison*, the Louisiana Purchase Treaty, a speech by President Abraham Lincoln delivered in the midst of the Civil War—these and other great documents in U.S. history breathe life into the great American story that followed the creation of the Charters.

The centerpiece of this presentation is, of course, the Charters themselves. As steward of these precious parchments, the National Archives has recently overseen the re-encasement of the Charters into the most scientifically advanced housing that preservation technology can provide. The Rotunda has been refurbished to allow for greater access, and the purpose of this grand space has been rededicated to telling the story of the Charters, their creation and their impact over the centuries. The true measure of success in the preservation of the Charters, however, is not what Americans see under glass, but the power of these words in their hearts.

"We have it in our power to begin the world over again. A situation, similar to the present, hath not happened since the days of Noah until now. The birthday of a new world is at hand."

THOMAS PAINE, FEBRUARY 14, 1776

INTRODUCTION

The simple truth at the heart of the American Revolution is that people are born with certain natural rights, including "Life, Liberty and the pursuit of Happiness," that do not come from presidents, kings, or charters. These and other rights of the American people are secured by this nation's founding documents: the Declaration of Independence, Constitution, and Bill of Rights. Known collectively as the Charters of Freedom, these three documents are on permanent display in the Rotunda of the National Archives Building in the nation's capital.

The Declaration announced to the world on July 4, 1776, that thirteen British colonies in North America were leaving Great Britain to form a separate nation. It specified how the King had trampled the people's rights. In justifying revolution, it gave voice to the ancient longing of the human soul—for freedom. The Constitution, drafted in 1787 after a hard-won victory in the War for Independence, codified the spirit of the Revolution into an ingenious practical scheme of government to promote the welfare of all its citizens. The Bill of Rights, added to the Constitution in 1791 as the first ten amendments, explicitly protected freedom of speech, of the press, of religion, and of assembly, among many other freedoms.

These documents were drafted in the heat of dramatic, fast-moving events. They represented a monumental achievement to the nation's Founders who believed their experiment in self-government held the promise of liberty for all mankind. The principles established in the Charters have bound the nation together through more than two centuries of growth and turmoil. American patriots of every generation have paid in blood to defend these principles.

The documents reproduced in this book chronicle the creation of the Charters and their impact on events in this country and around the world. They reveal the story of earlier generations of Americans who had both the vision to see a better world and the audacity to build it.

FROM LOYAL SUBJECTS TO TRAITOROUS REBELS
A ROYAL PROCLAMATION

In 1761, fifteen years before the United States of America burst onto the world stage with the Declaration of Independence, the American colonists were loyal British subjects who celebrated the coronation of their new King, George III. The colonies that stretched from present-day Maine to Georgia were distinctly English in character, although they had been settled by Scots, Welsh, Irish, Dutch, Swedes, Finns, Africans, French, Germans, and Swiss, as well as English.

As English men and women, the American colonists were heirs to the thirteenth-century English document, the Magna Carta, which established the principles that no one is above the law (not even the King), and that no one can take away certain rights. So in 1763, when the King began to assert his authority over the colonies to make them share the cost of the Seven Years' War that England had just fought and won, the English colonists protested by invoking their rights as free men and loyal subjects. It was only after a decade of repeated efforts on the part of the colonists to defend their rights that they resorted to armed conflict and, eventually, to the unthinkable— separation from the motherland.

"When the last dutiful & humble petition from Congress received no other Answer than declaring us Rebels, and out of the King's protection, I from that Moment look'd forward to a Revolution & Independence, as the only means of Salvation; and will risque the last Penny of my Fortune, & the last Drop of my Blood upon the Issue."

George Mason, October 2, 1778

Opposite page:
Portrait of George III, oil painting by Studio of Allan Ramsay, London, England, ca. 1770
Courtesy of Colonial Williamsburg Foundation, Williamsburg, Virginia

BY THE

KING,

A

PROCLAMATION,

For Suppressing Rebellion and Sedition.

GEORGE R.

HEREAS many of Our Subjects in divers Parts of Our Colonies and Plantations in *North America*, misled by dangerous and ill-designing Men, and forgetting the Allegiance which they owe to the Power that has protected and sustained them, after various disorderly Acts committed in Disturbance of the Public Peace, to the Obstruction of lawful Commerce, and to the Oppression of Our loyal Subjects carrying on the same, have at length proceeded to an open and avowed Rebellion, by arraying themselves in hostile Manner to withstand the Execution of the Law, and traitorously preparing, ordering, and levying War against Us.

AND whereas there is Reason to apprehend that such Rebellion hath been much promoted and encouraged by the traitorous Correspondence, Counsels, and Comfort of divers wicked and desperate Persons within this Realm: To the End therefore, that none of Our Subjects may neglect or violate their Duty through Ignorance thereof, or through any Doubt of the Protection which the Law will afford to their Loyalty and Zeal; We have thought fit, by and with the Advice of Our Privy Council, to issue this Our Royal Proclamation, hereby declaring that not only all Our Officers, Civil and Military, are obliged to exert their utmost Endeavours

due and
pondence with,
now in open Arms and
Colonies and Plantations in *Nor*
ment the Authors, Perpetrators, and Ab

justice; but
elonging are
ch Rebellion,
and Attempts

Officers, as well
ets, to use their
and to disclose and
they shall know to
se, that they tranf
er proper Officer
d carrying on Corre
abetting, the Perfo
ent within any of O
ring to condign Puni
aitorous Designs.

Given at Our Court at St. *James's*, the 23d Day of *Aug*
1775, in the Fifteenth Year of Our Reign.

God Save the King.

LONDON:
King's Most Excellent Maje

Opposite page:

A Proclamation by the King for Suppressing Rebellion and Sedition, August 23, 1775

By the spring of 1775, peaceful protest gave way to armed conflict at Lexington and Concord. Ignoring one last, futile plea for peace in a message known as the Olive Branch Petition, the King proclaimed in this document that the colonies stood in open rebellion to his authority and were subject to severe penalty, as was any British subject who failed to report the knowledge of rebellion or conspiracy. This document literally transformed loyal subjects into traitorous rebels.

National Archives, Records of the Continental and Confederation Congresses and the Constitutional Convention

"Pulling Down the Statue of George III at Bowling Green in Lower Manhattan," oil painting by William Walcutt, 1857

After hearing the news about independence on July 9, 1776, people in New York City celebrated by pulling down a statue of the King they had come to view as a tyrant.

Courtesy of Lafayette College Art Collection, Easton, Pennsylvania

The sole governing authority presiding over the tumultuous events of the American Revolution between 1774 and 1789 was a body known as Congress. With no power to regulate commerce or lay taxes, and with little ability to enforce any of its decisions, this group, representing the thirteen colonies, declared independence, conducted a war that defeated one of the greatest military powers of its day, and invented a new political entity that became

> ## *"Perhaps our Congress will be Exalted on a high Gallows."*
>
> Abraham Clark,
> signer of the Declaration of Independence,
> August 6, 1776

a sovereign independent nation. Its members pondered everything from the rightness of independence to the number of flints needed by the armies—sometimes with the enemy not far from their doorstep. Asserting their rights, they found themselves labeled as traitors.

The fifty-four men who composed the First Continental Congress represented different interests, religions, and regions; they held conflicting opinions on how best to restore their rights. Most did not know each other; some did not like each other. With no history of successful cooperation, they struggled to overcome their differences and, without knowing if the future held success or nooses for them all, they started down a long and perilous road toward independence.

Opposite page:
In the Old Raleigh Tavern, a correspondence committee at work, hand-colored engraving after an illustration by Howard Pyle, ca. 1896

While none of the members of the Continental Congress was actually tried for treason, fifteen who signed the Declaration of Independence had their homes destroyed, four were taken captive, and one spent the winter of 1776 in the woods, pursued by British soldiers who had burned his home. Before the end of the Revolutionary War, many of those who served in the Continental Congress suffered direct, personal consequences for their support of American liberty and independence. *Courtesy of The Granger Collection, New York, New York*

In Congress Nov. 9. 1775

Resolved That every member of this Congress considers himself under the ties of virtue, honor & love of his Country not to divulge directly or indirectly any matter or thing agitated or debated in Congress before the same shall have been determined, without leave of the Congress; nor any matter or thing determined in Congress which a majority of the Congress shall order to be kept secret, and that if any member shall violate this agreement he shall be expelled this Congress & deemed an enemy to the liberties of America & liable to be treated as such & that every member signify his consent to this agreement by signing the same.

Ja.s Duane
Lewis Morris
Fran.s Lewis
Wm Floyd
Rob.t R. Livingston jun.r
Henry Wisner
Steph.n Crane
Wil. Livingston
Tho.s Willing
And.w Allen
C. Humphreys
James Wilson

John Hancock
Josiah Bartlett
John Langdon
Thomas Cushing
Sam.l Adams
John Adams
Rob.t Treat Paine
Step. Hopkins
Sam.l Ward
Eliph.t Dyer
Roger Sherman
Silas Deane

B. Franklin
John Dickinson

The Agreement of Secrecy, November 9, 1775

Three months after the King declared every rebel a
traitor, and with a reward posted for the capture of
certain prominent rebel leaders, the delegates to
Congress adopted these strict rules of secrecy to protect the cause of American liberty and their own lives.

   This document bears the signatures of eighty-
seven delegates; thirty-nine signed on November 9,
and the other delegates signed as they reported to
Congress.

*National Archives, Records of the Continental and
Confederation Congresses and the Constitutional
Convention*

"We hold these truths to be self-evident,
that all men are created equal, that they
are endowed by their Creator with certain
unalienable Rights, that among these are
Life, Liberty and the pursuit of Happiness."

From the Declaration of Independence, adopted July 4, 1776

THE SPIRIT OF THE REVOLUTION

THE SPIRIT OF THE REVOLUTION
THE DECLARATION OF INDEPENDENCE

In June 1776, as Thomas Jefferson composed a draft of the Declaration of Independence from a second floor parlor of a bricklayer's house in Philadelphia, the largest invasion force in British military history was headed for New York Harbor. By the time the last of the fifty-six signers had affixed their names to the final edited document months later, an invading force of British soldiers had landed at Staten Island, the British had taken New York City, and the American patriots had committed themselves to a long and bloody struggle for liberty and independence.

The Declaration announced to the world the separation of the thirteen colonies from Great Britain and the establishment of the United States of America. It explained the causes of this radical move with a long list of charges against the King. In justifying the Revolution, it asserted a universal truth about human rights in words that have inspired downtrodden people through the ages and throughout the world to rise up against their oppressors.

Jefferson was not aiming at originality. The Declaration articulates the highest ideals of the Revolution, beliefs in liberty, equality, and the right to self-determination. Americans embraced a view of the world in which a person's position was determined, not by birth, rank, or title, but by talent, ability, and enterprise. It was a widely held view, circulated in newspapers, pamphlets, sermons, and schoolbooks; but it was Thomas Jefferson, the 33-year-old planter from Virginia, who put the immortal words to it.

Opposite page:
Mural detail showing Thomas Jefferson presenting a draft of the Declaration of Independence to John Hancock, President of the Continental Congress

In CONGRESS, July 4, 1776.

A DECLARATION

By the REPRESENTATIVES of the

UNITED STATES OF AMERICA,

In GENERAL CONGRESS ASSEMBLED.

WHEN in the Course of human Events, it becomes necessary for one People to dissolve the Political Bands which have connected them with another, and to assume among the Powers of the Earth, the separate and equal Station to which the Laws of Nature and of Nature's God entitle them, a decent Respect to the Opinions of Mankind requires that they should declare the causes which impel them to the Separation.

We hold these Truths to be self-evident, that all Men are created equal, that they are endowed by their Creator with certain unalienable Rights, that among these are Life, Liberty, and the Pursuit of Happiness—That to secure these Rights, Governments are instituted among Men, deriving their just Powers from the Consent of the Governed, that whenever any Form of Government becomes destructive of these Ends, it is the Right of the People to alter or to abolish it, and to institute new Government, laying its Foundation on such Principles, and organizing its Powers in such Form, as to them shall seem most likely to effect their Safety and Happiness. Prudence, indeed, will dictate that Governments long established should not be changed for light and transient Causes; and accordingly all Experience hath shewn, that Mankind are more disposed to suffer, while Evils are sufferable, than to right themselves by abolishing the Forms to which they are accustomed. But when a long Train of Abuses and Usurpations, pursuing invariably the same Object, evinces a Design to reduce them under absolute Despotism, it is their Right, it is their Duty, to throw off such Government, and to provide new Guards for their future Security. Such has been the patient Sufferance of these Colonies; and such is now the Necessity which constrains them to alter their former Systems of Government. The History of the present King of Great-Britain is a History of repeated Injuries and Usurpations, all having in direct Object the Establishment of an absolute Tyranny over these States. To prove this, let Facts be submitted to a candid World.

He has refused his Assent to Laws, the most wholesome and necessary for the public Good.

He has forbidden his Governors to pass Laws of immediate and pressing Importance, unless suspended in their Operation till his Assent should be obtained; and when so suspended, he has utterly neglected to attend to them.

He has refused to pass other Laws for the Accommodation of large Districts of People, unless those People would relinquish the Right of Representation in the Legislature, a Right inestimable to them, and formidable to Tyrants only.

He has called together Legislative Bodies at Places unusual, uncomfortable, and distant from the Depository of their public Records, for the sole Purpose of fatiguing them into Compliance with his Measures.

He has dissolved Representative Houses repeatedly, for opposing with manly Firmness his Invasions on the Rights of the People.

He has refused for a long Time, after such Dissolutions, to cause others to be elected; whereby the Legislative Powers, incapable of Annihilation, have returned to the People at large for their exercise; the State remaining in the mean time exposed to all the Dangers of Invasion from without, and Convulsions within.

He has endeavoured to prevent the Population of these States; for that Purpose obstructing the Laws for Naturalization of Foreigners; refusing to pass others to encourage their Migrations hither, and raising the Conditions of new Appropriations of Lands.

He has obstructed the Administration of Justice, by refusing his Assent to Laws for establishing Judiciary Powers.

He has made Judges dependent on his Will alone, for the Tenure of their Offices, and the Amount and Payment of their Salaries.

He has erected a Multitude of new Offices, and sent hither Swarms of Officers to harrass our People, and eat out their Substance.

He has kept among us, in Times of Peace, Standing Armies, without the consent of our Legislatures.

He has affected to render the Military independent of and superior to the Civil Power.

He has combined with others to subject us to a Jurisdiction foreign to our Constitution, and unacknowledged by our Laws; giving his Assent to their Acts of pretended Legislation:

For quartering large Bodies of Armed Troops among us:

For protecting them, by a mock Trial, from Punishment for any Murders which they should commit on the Inhabitants of these States:

For cutting off our Trade with all Parts of the World:

For imposing Taxes on us without our Consent:

For depriving us, in many Cases, of the Benefits of Trial by Jury:

For transporting us beyond Seas to be tried for pretended Offences:

For abolishing the free System of English Laws in a neighbouring Province, establishing therein an arbitrary Government, and enlarging its Boundaries, so as to render it at once an Example and fit Instrument for introducing the same absolute Rule into these Colonies:

For taking away our Charters, abolishing our most valuable Laws, and altering fundamentally the Forms of our Governments:

For suspending our own Legislatures, and declaring themselves invested with Power to legislate for us in all Cases whatsoever.

He has abdicated Government here, by declaring us out of his Protection and waging War against us.

He has plundered our Seas, ravaged our Coasts, burnt our Towns, and destroyed the Lives of our People.

He is, at this Time, transporting large Armies of foreign Mercenaries to compleat the Works of Death, Desolation, and Tyranny, already begun with circumstances of Cruelty and Perfidy, scarcely paralleled in the most barbarous Ages, and totally unworthy the Head of a civilized Nation.

He has constrained our fellow Citizens taken Captive on the high Seas to bear Arms against their Country, to become the Executioners of their Friends and Brethren, or to fall themselves by their Hands.

He has excited domestic Insurrections amongst us, and has endeavoured to bring on the Inhabitants of our Frontiers, the merciless Indian Savages, whose known Rule of Warfare, is an undistinguished Destruction, of all Ages, Sexes and Conditions.

In every stage of these Oppressions we have Petitioned for Redress in the most humble Terms: Our repeated Petitions have been answered only by repeated Injury. A Prince, whose Character is thus marked by every act which may define a Tyrant, is unfit to be the Ruler of a free People.

Nor have we been wanting in Attentions to our British Brethren. We have warned them from Time to Time of Attempts by their Legislature to extend an unwarrantable Jurisdiction over us. We have reminded them of the Circumstances of our Emigration and Settlement here. We have appealed to their native Justice and Magnanimity, and we have conjured them by the Ties of our common Kindred to disavow these Usurpations, which, would inevitably interrupt our Connections and Correspondence. They too have been deaf to the Voice of Justice and of Consanguinity. We must, therefore, acquiesce in the Necessity, which denounces our Separation, and hold them, as we hold the rest of Mankind, Enemies in War, in Peace, Friends.

We, therefore, the Representatives of the UNITED STATES OF AMERICA, in GENERAL CONGRESS, Assembled, appealing to the Supreme Judge of the World for the Rectitude of our Intentions, do, in the Name, and by Authority of the good People of these Colonies, solemnly Publish and Declare, That these United Colonies are, and of Right ought to be, FREE AND INDEPENDENT STATES; that they are absolved from all Allegiance to the British Crown, and that all political Connection between them and the State of Great-Britain, is and ought to be totally dissolved; and that as FREE AND INDEPENDENT STATES, they have full Power to levy War, conclude Peace, contract Alliances, establish Commerce, and to do all other Acts and Things which INDEPENDENT STATES may of right do. And for the support of this Declaration, with a firm Reliance on the Protection of divine Providence, we mutually pledge to each other our Lives, our Fortunes, and our sacred Honor.

Signed by ORDER and in BEHALF of the CONGRESS,

JOHN HANCOCK, PRESIDENT.

ATTEST.
CHARLES THOMSON, SECRETARY.

PHILADELPHIA: PRINTED BY JOHN DUNLAP.

A N.W. VIEW OF THE STATE HOUSE IN PHILADELPHIA taken 1778

Opposite page:
First printing of the Declaration of Independence, produced during the night of July 4–5, 1776

John Dunlap, the official printer for the Continental Congress, produced the first printing of the Declaration on the night of July 4–5. These copies, known as the Dunlap Broadsides, were delivered to Congress on the morning of July 5. This one was inserted into the "rough journal" of the Continental Congress in the July 4 entry.

It is not known how many copies Dunlap printed on the night of July 4. Twenty-five copies are known to exist.

National Archives, Records of the Continental and Confederation Congresses and the Constitutional Convention

"A N.W. View of the State House in Philadelphia taken 1778," engraving by James B. Trenchard after Charles Willson Peale, 1787

Courtesy of the Library of Congress, Washington, DC

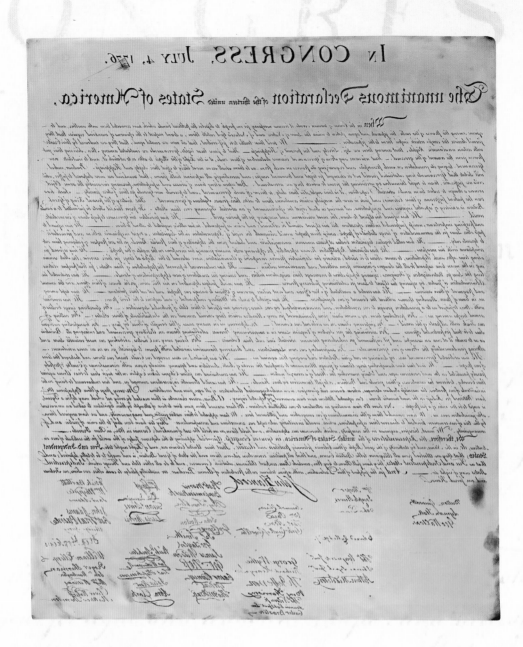

Copperplate of the Declaration of Independence, completed 1823

As early as 1817, Secretary of State Richard Rush noted the effects that "the hand of time" had had on the Declaration of Independence. In 1820 Secretary of State John Quincy Adams commissioned William F. Stone, a Washington, DC, printer and engraver, to make a facsimile of the document—its text, lettering, and signatures. Three years later, Stone completed a copperplate of the Declaration—nearly life-size—and turned it over to the Department of State which had two hundred copies printed on parchment.

In 1976, printers from the Bureau of Engraving and Printing struck seven additional prints from Stone's copperplate to commemorate the Bicentennial of the American Revolution.

National Archives, General Records of the Department of State

Print of the Declaration of Independence made in 1976 for the nation's two hundredth anniversary

On July 4, 1776, Congress completed its editing of the document, reducing the text by 25 percent ("mutilations" is what Jefferson called it), and formally adopted the Declaration. On July 19, Congress ordered that a formal copy of the Declaration be prepared for members to sign. On August 2, the final parchment was presented to Congress and the signing began.

John Hancock, the President of Congress was the first to sign; his signature is larger than any other on the page and directly centered below the text. The signatures of the other delegates are arranged from right to left, according to the geographic locations of their states, beginning with New Hampshire, the northernmost, on the right, and ending with Georgia, the southernmost, on the left. Eventually, fifty-six delegates signed, although not all of them were present on August 2; some who were present for the vote on July 4 never signed.

This print, made from the copperplate, shows what the original parchment looked like when it was newly signed by the delegates of the Continental Congress in 1776.

National Archives, Unaccessioned Record

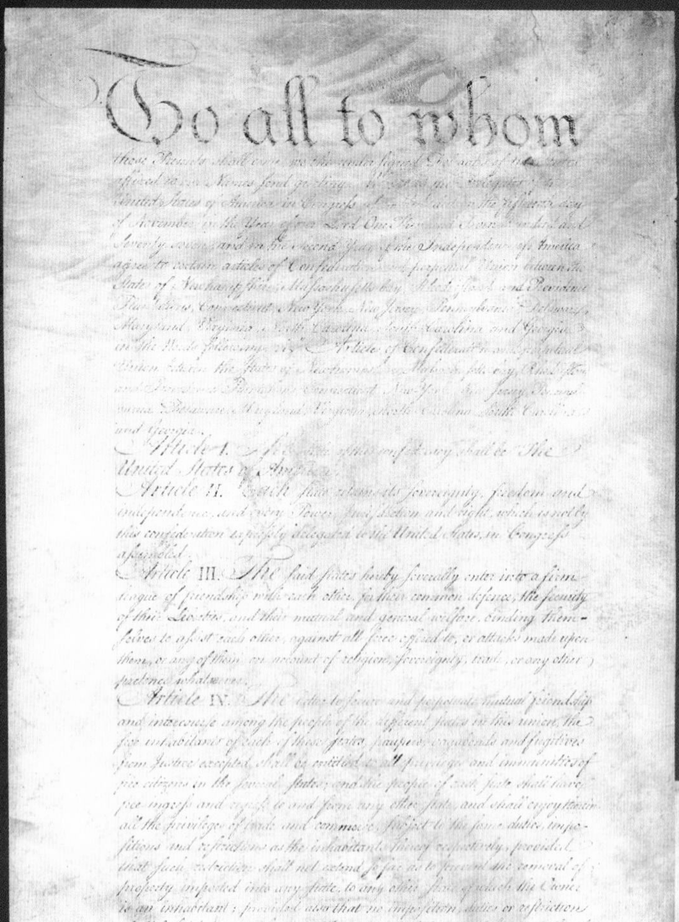
To all to whom

Article I. The Stile of this confederacy shall be "The United States of America".

Article II. Each state retains its sovereignty, freedom and independence, and every Power, Jurisdiction and right, which is not by this confederation expressly delegated to the United States, in Congress assembled.

Article III. The said states hereby severally enter into a firm league of friendship with each other, for their common defence, the security of their Liberties, and their mutual and general welfare, binding themselves to assist each other, against all force offered to, or attacks made upon them, or any of them, on account of religion, sovereignty, trade, or any other pretence whatever.

Article IV. The better to secure and perpetuate mutual friendship and intercourse among the people of the different states in this union, the free inhabitants of each of these states, paupers, vagabonds and fugitives from Justice excepted, shall be entitled to all privileges and immunities of free citizens in the several states; and the people of each state shall have free ingress and regress to and from any other state, and shall enjoy therein all the privileges of trade and commerce, subject to the same duties, impositions and restrictions as the inhabitants thereof respectively, provided that such restriction shall not extend so far as to prevent the removal of property imported into any state, to any other state of which the Owner is an inhabitant; provided also that no imposition, duties or restriction shall be laid by any state, on the property of the united states, or either of them.

If any Person guilty of, or charged with treason, felony, or other high misdemeanor in any state, shall flee from Justice, and be found in any of the united states, he shall upon demand of the Governor or executive power, of the state from which he fled, be delivered up and removed to the state having jurisdiction of his offence.

Full faith and credit shall be given in each of these states to the records, acts and judicial proceedings of the courts and magistrates of every other state.

Article V. For the more convenient management of the general interests of the united states, delegates shall be annually appointed in such manner as the legislature of each state shall direct, to meet in Congress on the first Monday in November, in every year, with a power reserved to each state, to recal its delegates, or any of them, at any time within the year, and to send others in their stead, for the remainder of the Year.

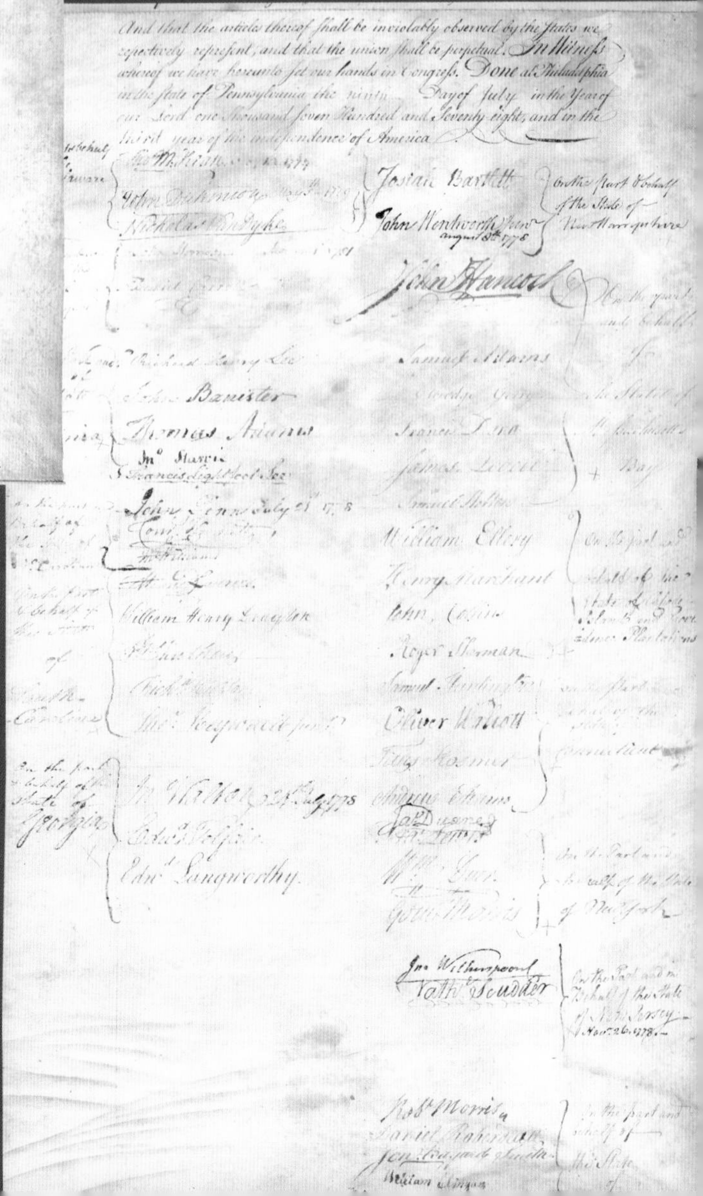
And that the articles thereof shall be inviolably observed by the states we respectively represent, and that the union shall be perpetual. In Witness whereof we have hereunto set our hands in Congress. Done at Philadelphia in the state of Pennsylvania the ninth Day of July in the Year of our Lord one Thousand seven Hundred and Seventy eight, and in the third year of the independence of America.

Josiah Bartlett
John Wentworth Junr August 8th 1778
On the part & behalf of the State of New Hampshire

John Hancock
Samuel Adams
William Ellery
Henry Marchant
John Collins
Roger Sherman
Samuel Huntington
Oliver Wolcott
Jno Witherspoon
Nath. Scudder
On the Part and in Behalf of the State of New Jersey. Novr. 26, 1778.
Robt Morris

John Dickinson
Nicholas Van Dyke
Richard Henry Lee
John Banister
Thomas Adams
Jno Harvie
Francis Lightfoot Lee
John Penn July 21st 1778
William Henry Drayton
Edwd Telfair
Edwd Langworthy

Articles of Confederation, ratified March 1, 1781

During the eight years that the Articles were in effect, the United States fought and won the War for Independence, negotiated a brilliant peace settlement, and created a functioning bureaucracy. The crowning achievement of the government under the Articles of Confederation was the 1787 Northwest Ordinance, which provided for the orderly expansion of a republican form of government into the western territories.

This document consists of six sheets of parchment stitched together. The last sheet bears the signatures of delegates from all thirteen states.

National Archives, Records of the Continental and Confederation Congresses and the Constitutional Convention

> *"We have it in our power to begin the world over again. A situation, similar to the present, hath not happened since the days of Noah until now. The birthday of a new world is at hand."*

THOMAS PAINE, FEBRUARY 14, 1776

THE FIRST CONSTITUTION
THE ARTICLES OF CONFEDERATION

Throwing off the British monarchy on July 4, 1776, left the United States with no central government. It had to design and install a new government—and quickly. As early as May 1776, Congress advised each of the colonies to draw up plans for state governments; by 1780, all thirteen states had adopted written constitutions. In June 1776, the Continental Congress began to work on a plan for a central government. It took five years for it to be approved, first by members of Congress, and then by the states. The first attempt at a constitution for the United States was called the Articles of Confederation.

This first constitution was composed by a body that directed most of its attention to fighting and winning the War for Independence. It came into being at a time when Americans had a deep-seated fear of a central authority and long-standing loyalty to the state in which they lived and often called their "country." Ultimately, the Articles of Confederation proved unwieldy and inadequate to resolve the issues that faced the United States in its earliest years; but in granting any Federal powers to a central authority—the Confederation Congress—this document marked a crucial step toward nationhood. The Articles of Confederation were in force from March 1, 1781, until March 4, 1789, when the present Constitution came into effect.

Assembly Room, Pennsylvania State House, later named Independence Hall, meeting place of Congress, photograph by Robin Miller, 2001

The Declaration of Independence, Articles of Confederation, and U.S. Constitution were signed in this room.
Courtesy of Independence National Historical Park, Philadelphia, Pennsylvania

"Am I Not a Man and a Brother?,"
woodcut, ca. 1837
Courtesy of the Library of Congress,
Washington, DC

The Revolution's ideals of liberty and equality existed side by side with the brutal realities of human slavery. By the time of the Revolution, slavery existed in all the colonies, slaves made up 20 percent of the population, and their labor had become a vital contribution to the physical and economic development of the colonies. The existence of slavery created tensions that would strain the integrity of the United States for many decades to come.

The Society of Friends, a religious group also known as the Quakers, formed the first formal antislavery society in 1775. Throughout the Revolution, as the states struggled to find common ground, the issue of slavery was so divisive that it threatened to shatter their fragile union. Some prominent leaders of the Revolution raised their voices to oppose slavery on moral grounds. Slaves and free Africans embraced the principles of liberty and equality embedded in the Declaration as their own best hope for freedom and better treatment. Many, fighting as soldiers in the American armies, helped to defeat the British while earning their freedom and gaining the respect and gratitude of some whites. And clinging to their own understanding of "all men are created equal," they pushed the country closer to living out the full promise of its words.

"I beheld a middle aged African raised and exposed on one of the stalls in the shambles of Philadelphia market at Public Sale, as a Slave for life! and this is the capital of Pennsylvania, a land high in the profession of Liberty and Christianity."

Colonist quoted in *Pennsylvania Packet*, a Philadelphia newspaper, February 7, 1774

To the United States in Congress assembled

The Address of the People called Quakers

Being through the favour of Divine Providence met as usual at this season in our annual Assembly to promote the cause of Piety and Virtue, We find with great satisfaction our well meant endeavours for the relief of an oppressed part of our fellow Men have been so far blessed, that those of them who have been held in bondage by Members of our Religious Society are generally restored to freedom, their natural and just right.

Commiserating the afflicted State into which the Inhabitants of Africa are very deeply involved by many Professors of the mild and benign doctrines of the Gospel, and affected with a sincere concern for the essential Good of our Country, We conceive it our indispensible duty to revive the lamentable grievance of that oppressed people in your view as an interesting subject evidently claiming the serious attention of those who are entrusted with the powers of Government, as Guardians of the common rights of Mankind, and advocates for liberty.

We have long beheld with sorrow the complicated evils produced by an unrighteous commerce which subjects many thousands of the human species to the deplorable State of Slavery

The Restoration of Peace and restraint to the effusion of human Blood we are persuaded excite in the minds of many, of all Christian denominations gratitude and thankfulness to the all wise Controuler of human events; but we have grounds to fear, that some forgetful of the days of Distress are prompted from avaricious motives to renew the iniquitous trade for Slaves to the African Coasts, contrary to every humane and righteous consideration; and in opposition to the solemn declarations often repeated in favour of universal liberty, thereby increasing the too general torrent of Corruption and licentiousness, and laying a foundation for future Calamities.

We therefore earnestly sollicit your Christian interposition to discourage and prevent so obvious an Evil, in such manner as under the influence of Divine Wisdom you shall see meet.

Signed in and on behalf of our Yearly Meeting held in Philadelphia for Pennsylvania, New Jersey, and Delaware, and the Western parts of Maryland and Virginia, dated the fourth day of the tenth Month 1783.

Isaac Zane
John Reynell
Thos. Ross
John Price Jun
Hugh Roberts
Joseph Dewees
Isaac Pickering
William Harvey
Joshua Morris
Daniel Haviland

Joshua Brown
George Evans
Thomas Watson
Anthony Benezet
James Thornton
Warner Mifflin
Samuel Emlen jun
Daniel Byrnes
Ro. Dillwyn

Sam. Pemberton
Jacob Lindley
Thomas Lightfoot
Mark Reeve
William Savery Jun
John Hoskins
George Churchman
Thomas Methews

Wm. Kersey
David Roper
Benj. Swett
Owen Jones
Eli. Yarnall
David Evans
Silas Downing
Aaron Lancaster

Opposite page:

Quaker petition to Congress, October 4, 1783

As early as 1688, the Quakers had been expressing their opposition to slavery, which they considered to be sinful. This petition, asking that Congress end the slave trade, was signed by more than five hundred Quakers. Citing the Declaration of Independence, the petition states that the slave trade exists "... in opposition to the solemn declaration often repeated in favor of universal liberty." The petition was read in Congress on October 8 and subsequently tabled.

National Archives, Records of the Continental and Confederation Congresses and the Constitutional Convention

"Elizabeth 'Mumbet' Freeman," watercolor by Susan Anne Livingston Ridley Sedgwick, 1811

In states where slaves were considered as persons before the law, they sued for, and sometimes won, their freedom in the courts. Elizabeth Freeman achieved freedom after petitioning Massachusetts in 1781. "Anytime while I was a slave," she said, "if one minute's freedom had been offered to me, and I had been told I must die at the end of that minute, I would have taken it—just to stand one minute . . . on God's airth a free woman. I would."

Courtesy Massachusetts Historical Society, Boston

Eleven years after the Declaration of Independence announced the birth of the United States, the survival of the young country seemed in doubt. The War for Independence had been won, but economic depression, social unrest, interstate rivalries, and foreign intrigue appeared to be unraveling the fragile confederation. In early 1787, Congress called for a special convention of all the states to revise the Articles of Confederation. On September 17, 1787, after four months of secret meetings, the delegates to the

---

"[The Constitution of the United States] was not, like the fabled Goddess of Wisdom, the offspring of a single brain. It ought to be regarded as the work of many heads and many hands."

James Madison, March 10, 1834

Constitutional Convention emerged from their Philadelphia meetingroom with an entirely new plan of government—the U.S. Constitution—that they hoped would ensure the survival of the experiment they had launched in 1776.

They proposed a strong central government made up of three branches: legislative, executive, and judicial; each would be perpetually restrained by a sophisticated set of checks and balances. They reached compromises on the issue of slavery that left its final resolution to future generations. As for ratification, they devised a procedure that maximized the odds: the Constitution would be enacted when it was ratified by nine, not thirteen, states. The Framers knew they had not created a perfect plan, but it could be revised. The Constitution has been amended twenty-seven times and stands today as the longest-lasting written national constitution in the world.

Opposite page:
Mural detail showing James Madison
offering the final draft of the
Constitution to George Washington

"Washington as Statesman at the Constitutional Convention," oil painting by Junius Brutus Stearns, 1856

In drafting the Constitution, the delegates consulted the wisdom of the ages, sifting through the contemporary political tracts of their own day, as well as the histories of ancient civilizations. They understood power to be corrupting and humans to be subject to their worst instincts.

The debates inside the meetingroom were heated and contentious. The delegates examined every phrase of the constitution through the prism of the conflicting interests they represented: large states and small states, states with commercially-based economies versus states with slave-based agricultural economies. History, political theory, their own interests, and devotion to the American experiment, all informed their thinking as they hammered out a practical scheme of government.
Courtesy of the Virginia Museum of Fine Arts, Richmond, Virginia, Gift of Edgar William and Bernice Chrysler Garbisch, 1950

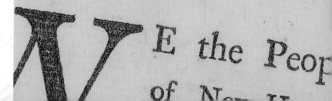

W E the People of the States of New-Hampfhire, Maffachufetts, Rhode-Ifland and Providence Plantations, Connecticut, New-York, New-Jerfey, Pennfylvania, Delaware, Maryland, Virginia, North-Carolina, South-Carolina, and Georgia, do ordain, declare and eftablifh the following Conftitution for the Government of Ourfelves and our Pofterity.

ARTICLE I.

The ftile of this Government fhall be, " The United States of America."

II.

The Government fhall confift of fupreme legiflative, executive and judicial powers.

III.

The legiflative power fhall be vefted in a Congrefs, to confift of two feparate and diftinct bodies of men, a Houfe of Reprefentatives, and a Senate; ~~each of which fhall, in all cafes, have a negative on the other. The Legiflature fhall meet on the firft Monday in December in every year.~~

The Legislature fhall meet at least once in every year and that meeting fhall be on the firft Monday in December unlefs a different day fhall be appointed by Law.

IV.

Sect. 1. The Members of the Houfe of Reprefentatives fhall be chofen every fecond year, by the people of the feveral States comprehended within this Union. The qualifications of the electors fhall be the fame, from time to time, as thofe of the electors in the feveral States, of the moft numerous branch of their own legiflatures.

Sect. 2. Every Member of the Houfe of Reprefentatives fhall be of the age of twenty-five years at leaft; fhall have been a citizen in the United States for at leaft [...] years before his election; and fhall be, at the time of his election, [...] of the State in which he fhall be chofen.

Sect. 3. The Houfe of Reprefentatives fhall, at its firft formation, and until the number of citizens and inhabitants fhall be taken in the manner herein after defcribed, confift of fixty-five Members, of whom three fhall be chofen in New-Hampfhire, eight in Maffachufetts, one in Rhode-Ifland and Providence Plantations, five in Connecticut, fix in New-York, four in New-Jerfey, eight in Pennfylvania, one in Delaware, fix in Maryland, ten in Virginia, five in North-Carolina, five in South-Carolina, and three in Georgia.

Sect. 4. As the proportions of numbers in the different States will alter from time to time; as fome of the States may hereafter be divided; as others may be enlarged by addition of territory; as two or more States may be united; as new States will be erected within the limits of the United States, the Legiflature fhall, in each of thefe cafes, regulate the number of reprefentatives by the number of inhabitants, according to the [...] the rate of one for every forty thoufand. *Provided that every State fhall have at least One representative.*

Sect. 5. All bills for raifing or appropriating money, and for fixing the falaries of the officers of government, fhall originate in the Houfe of Reprefentatives, and fhall not be altered or amended by the Senate. No money fhall be drawn from the public Treafury, but in purfuance of appropriations that fhall originate in the Houfe of Reprefentatives.

Sect. 6. The Houfe of Reprefentatives fhall have the fole power of impeachment. It fhall choofe its Speaker and other officers.

Sect. 7. Vacancies in the Houfe of Reprefentatives fhall be fupplied by writs of election from the executive authority of the State, in the reprefentation from which they fhall happen.

V.

First printed draft of the Constitution, August 6, 1787, selected pages

Fifty-five delegates from twelve of the thirteen states attended sessions of the Convention (Rhode Island refused to participate). George Washington, a delegate from Virginia, was unanimously elected President of the Convention on May 25, 1787.

This was George Washington's own working copy with his annotations. Here, the preamble lists each of the thirteen states by name; the preamble of the next printed draft of the constitution, first reported on September 12, began "We, the people of the United States, . . ." signaling one of the most fundamental precepts of the Constitution: the primacy of the national government over the states.

National Archives, Records of the Continental and Confederation Congresses and the Constitutional Convention

**James Madison, oil painting by
Charles Willson Peale, ca. 1792**

At the Constitutional Convention, the
role of Virginia delegate James Madison
was so critical that he is known as the
"Father of the Constitution." Later,
as a member of the House of
Representatives from Virginia, he
introduced in the House amendments
to the Constitution designed to protect
individual liberties. His proposals
became the basis of the Bill of Rights.
*Courtesy of Gilcrease Museum, Tulsa,
Oklahoma*

THE BILL OF RIGHTS
THE FIRST TEN AMENDMENTS
TO THE CONSTITUTION

Freedom of speech, freedom of the press, freedom of assembly, the right to a fair and speedy trial—the ringing phrases that inventory some of Americans' most treasured personal freedoms—were not initially part of the U.S. Constitution. At the Constitutional Convention, the proposal to include a bill of rights was considered and defeated. The Bill of Rights was added to the Constitution as the first ten amendments on December 15, 1791.

The fact that the Constitution did not include a bill of rights specifically to protect Americans' hard-won rights sparked the most heated debates during the ratification process. To the Federalists, those who favored the Constitution, a bill of rights was unnecessary because the Federal Government was limited in its powers and could not interfere with the rights of the people or the states; also, most states had bills of rights. To the Anti-Federalists, those who opposed the Constitution, the prospect of establishing a strong central government without an explicit list of rights guaranteed to the people was unthinkable. Throughout the ratification process, individuals and state ratification conventions called for the adoption of a bill of rights.

The First Federal Congress took up the question of a bill of rights almost immediately. Congress proposed twelve amendments to the states. Ten of these were added to the Constitution on December 15, 1791.

"The sacred rights of mankind are not to be rummaged for,
among old parchments, or musty records.
They are written, as with a sun beam in the whole
volume of human nature, by the hand of the divinity itself;
and can never be erased or obscured by mortal power."

Alexander Hamilton, 1775

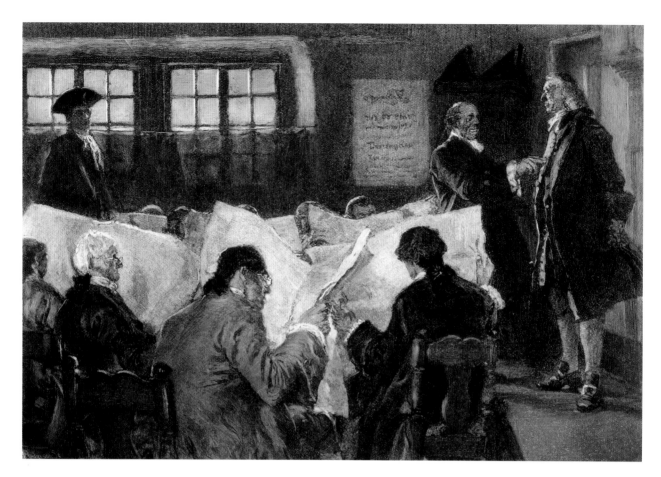

In the Reading Room of an 18th-century New York Coffee House, hand-colored engraving after an illustration by Howard Pyle, ca. 1890

The fate of the proposed constitution was decided in the state ratifying conventions (nine states had to ratify for the Constitution to take effect), but it was the subject of intense debates everywhere—in homes, taverns, coffee houses, and newspapers. By the time New Hampshire became the ninth state to ratify in June 1788, it had become clear that the people of the United States demanded a bill of rights.

Courtesy of The Granger Collection, New York, New York

The Committees of the two Houses appointed to confer on their different votes on the Amendments proposed by the Senate to the Resolution proposing Amendments to the Constitution, and disagreed to by the House of Representatives, have had a conference, and have agreed that it will be proper for the House of Representatives to agree to the said Amendments proposed by the Senate, with an Amendment to their fifth Amendment so that the third Article shall read as follows "Congress shall make no law respecting an establishment of Religion, or prohibiting the free exercise thereof; or abridging the freedom of speech, or of the Press; or the right of the people peaceably to assemble and to petition the Government for a redress of grievances;" — And with an Amendment to the fourteenth Amendment proposed by the Senate so that the eighth Article, as numbered in the Amendments proposed by the Senate, shall read as follows "In all criminal prosecutions, the accused shall enjoy the right to a speedy & publick trial by an impartial jury of the district wherein the crime shall have been committed, as the district shall have been previously ascertained by law, and to be informed of the

"the nature and cause of the accusation; to be confronted with the witnesses against him; and to have compulsory process for obtaining witnesses against him in his favour, & have the assistance of counsel for his defence;"

The Committee were also of opinion it would be proper for both Houses to agree to amend the first Article, by striking out the word "less" in the last line but one and inserting in its place the word "more", and accordingly recommend that the said Article be reconsidered for that purpose.

Report of the Conference Committee appointed to settle the differences between the House and Senate versions of the proposed bill of rights, September 24, 1789

This report, in the handwriting of Connecticut Senator Oliver Ellsworth, shows the final wording of what would become the First Amendment to the Constitution.
National Archives, Records of the U.S. Senate, reproduced with the permission of the U.S. Senate

Congress OF TH

begun and held at th

Wednesday the fourth of March,

4 THE Conventions of a number of the

further declaratory and restrictive clauses should be added: And

RESOLVED by the Senate

ing Articles be proposed to the Legislatures of the several States,

alid to all intents and purposes, as part of the said Constitution

ARTICLES in addition to, and

suant to the fifth Article of the original Constitution.

first enumeration required by the first Article of the Constitution, a

FIRST TEN AMENDMENTS TO THE CONSTITUTION

Bill of Rights, ratified December 15, 1791, detail

AMENDMENT I

Congress shall make no law respecting an establishment of religion, or prohibiting the free exercise thereof; or abridging the freedom of speech, or of the press; or the right of the people peaceably to assemble, and to petition the Government for a redress of grievances.

AMENDMENT II

A well regulated Militia, being necessary to the security of a free State, the right of the people to keep and bear Arms, shall not be infringed.

AMENDMENT III

No Soldier shall, in time of peace be quartered in any house, without the consent of the Owner, nor in time of war, but in a manner to be prescribed by law.

AMENDMENT IV

The right of the people to be secure in their persons, houses, papers, and effects, against unreasonable searches and seizures, shall not be violated, and no Warrants shall issue, but upon probable cause, supported by Oath or affirmation, and particularly describing the place to be searched, and the persons or things to be seized.

AMENDMENT V

No person shall be held to answer for a capital, or otherwise infamous crime, unless on a presentment or indictment of a Grand Jury, except in cases arising in the land or naval forces, or in the Militia, when in actual service in time of War or public danger; nor shall any person be subject for the same offence to be twice put in jeopardy of life or limb; nor shall be compelled in any criminal case to be a witness against himself, nor be deprived of life, liberty, or property, without due process of law; nor shall private property be taken for public use, without just compensation.

AMENDMENT VI

In all criminal prosecutions, the accused shall enjoy the right to a speedy and public trial, by an impartial jury of the State and district wherein the crime shall have been committed, which district shall have been previously ascertained by law, and to be informed of the nature and cause of the accusation; to be confronted with the witnesses against him; to have compulsory process for obtaining witnesses in his favor, and to have the Assistance of Counsel for his defence.

AMENDMENT VII

In Suits at common law, where the value in controversy shall exceed twenty dollars, the right of trial by jury shall be preserved, and no fact tried by a jury, shall be otherwise re-examined in any Court of the United States, than according to the rules of the common law.

AMENDMENT VIII

Excessive bail shall not be required, nor excessive fines imposed, nor cruel and unusual punishments inflicted.

AMENDMENT IX

The enumeration in the Constitution, of certain rights, shall not be construed to deny or disparage others retained by the people.

AMENDMENT X

The powers not delegated to the United States by the Constitution, nor prohibited by it to the States, are reserved to the States respectively, or to the people.

Declaration of Independence

THE CHARTERS OF FREEDOM

Declaration of Independence, adopted July 4, 1776

Timothy Matlack, an assistant to the Secretary of the
Continental Congress engrossed, or transcribed, this document in a large, clear hand. It was signed on August 2, 1776, by
John Hancock, President of the Continental Congress, and by
other members present. Most of those who were absent that
day signed later. Eventually, fifty-six members of the
Continental Congress signed this document. It is the nation's
official, record copy and is on permanent display.

This original, signed document shows signs of fading and
aging. As a symbol of the Revolution's highest ideals, it has
been lovingly handled and proudly displayed over many years.
Its present condition is evidence, not of indifference or neglect—but of extreme devotion. To preserve it for future generations, it is sealed in the most scientifically advanced housing
that preservation technology can provide.

National Archives, General Records of the U.S. Government

pages 56–59
Constitution of the United States, adopted September 17, 1787

On September 15, 1787, the delegates to the Constitutional Convention
unanimously agreed to the Constitution. On September 16–17, Jacob
Shallus, assistant to the Secretary of the Convention, engrossed the
document on these four pieces of parchment. On September 17, this
document was signed by George Washington, President of the
Convention, and thirty-eight delegates still in attendance. All four
pages are on permanent display.

National Archives, General Records of the U.S. Government

We the People

of the United States, in order to form a more perfect Union, establish Justice, insure domestic Tranquility, provide for the common defence, promote the general Welfare, and secure the Blessings of Liberty to ourselves and our Posterity, do ordain and establish this Constitution for the United States of America.

Article. 1.

Section. 1. All legislative Powers herein granted shall be vested in a Congress of the United States, which shall consist of a Senate and House of Representatives.

Section. 2. The House of Representatives shall be composed of Members chosen every second Year by the People of the several States, and the Electors in each State shall have the Qualifications requisite for Electors of the most numerous Branch of the State Legislature.

No Person shall be a Representative who shall not have attained to the Age of twenty five Years, and been seven Years a Citizen of the United States, and who shall not, when elected, be an Inhabitant of that State in which he shall be chosen.

Representatives and direct Taxes shall be apportioned among the several States which may be included within this Union, according to their respective Numbers, which shall be determined by adding to the whole Number of free Persons, including those bound to Service for a Term of Years, and excluding Indians not taxed, three fifths of all other Persons. The actual Enumeration shall be made within three Years after the first Meeting of the Congress of the United States, and within every subsequent Term of ten Years, in such Manner as they shall by Law direct. The Number of Representatives shall not exceed one for every thirty Thousand, but each State shall have at Least one Representative; and until such enumeration shall be made, the State of New Hampshire shall be entitled to chuse three, Massachusetts eight, Rhode-Island and Providence Plantations one, Connecticut five, New-York six, New Jersey four, Pennsylvania eight, Delaware one, Maryland six, Virginia ten, North Carolina five, South Carolina five, and Georgia three.

When vacancies happen in the Representation from any State, the Executive Authority thereof shall issue Writs of Election to fill such Vacancies.

The House of Representatives shall chuse their Speaker and other Officers; and shall have the sole Power of Impeachment.

Section. 3. The Senate of the United States shall be composed of two Senators from each State, chosen by the Legislature thereof, for six Years; and each Senator shall have one Vote.

Immediately after they shall be assembled in Consequence of the first Election, they shall be divided as equally as may be into three Classes. The Seats of the Senators of the first Class shall be vacated at the Expiration of the second Year, of the second Class at the Expiration of the fourth Year, and of the third Class at the Expiration of the sixth Year, so that one third may be chosen every second Year; and if Vacancies happen by Resignation, or otherwise, during the Recess of the Legislature of any State, the Executive thereof may make temporary Appointments until the next Meeting of the Legislature, which shall then fill such Vacancies.

No Person shall be a Senator who shall not have attained to the Age of thirty Years, and been nine Years a Citizen of the United States, and who shall not, when elected, be an Inhabitant of that State for which he shall be chosen.

The Vice President of the United States shall be President of the Senate, but shall have no Vote, unless they be equally divided.

The Senate shall chuse their other Officers, and also a President pro tempore, in the Absence of the Vice President, or when he shall exercise the Office of President of the United States.

The Senate shall have the sole Power to try all Impeachments. When sitting for that Purpose, they shall be on Oath or Affirmation. When the President of the United States is tried, the Chief Justice shall preside: And no Person shall be convicted without the Concurrence of two thirds of the Members present.

Judgment in Cases of Impeachment shall not extend further than to removal from Office, and disqualification to hold and enjoy any Office of honor, Trust or Profit under the United States: but the Party convicted shall nevertheless be liable and subject to Indictment, Trial, Judgment and Punishment, according to Law.

Section. 4. The Times, Places and Manner of holding Elections for Senators and Representatives, shall be prescribed in each State by the Legislature thereof; but the Congress may at any time by Law make or alter such Regulations, except as to the Places of chusing Senators.

The Congress shall assemble at least once in every Year, and such Meeting shall be on the first Monday in December, unless they shall by Law appoint a different Day.

Section. 5. Each House shall be the Judge of the Elections, Returns and Qualifications of its own Members, and a Majority of each shall constitute a Quorum to do Business; but a smaller Number may adjourn from day to day, and may be authorized to compel the Attendance of absent Members, in such Manner, and under such Penalties as each House may provide.

Each House may determine the Rules of its Proceedings, punish its Members for disorderly Behaviour, and, with the Concurrence of two thirds, expel a Member.

Each House shall keep a Journal of its Proceedings, and from time to time publish the same, excepting such Parts as may in their Judgment require Secrecy; and the Yeas and Nays of the Members of either House on any question shall, at the Desire of one fifth of those Present, be entered on the Journal.

Neither House, during the Session of Congress, shall, without the Consent of the other, adjourn for more than three days, nor to any other Place than that in which the two Houses shall be sitting.

Section. 6. The Senators and Representatives shall receive a Compensation for their Services, to be ascertained by Law, and paid out of the Treasury of the United States. They shall in all Cases, except Treason, Felony and Breach of the Peace, be privileged from Arrest during their Attendance at the Session of their respective Houses, and in going to and returning from the same; and for any Speech or Debate in either House, they shall not be questioned in any other Place.

No Senator or Representative shall, during the Time for which he was elected, be appointed to any civil Office under the Authority of the United States, which shall have been created, or the Emoluments whereof shall have been encreased during such time; and no Person holding any Office under the United States, shall be a Member of either House during his Continuance in Office.

Section. 7. All Bills for raising Revenue shall originate in the House of Representatives; but the Senate may propose or concur with Amendments as on other Bills.

Every Bill which shall have passed the House of Representatives and the Senate, shall, before it become a Law, be presented to the President of the

United States; If he approve he shall sign it, but if not he shall return it, with his Objections to that House in which it shall have originated, who shall enter the Objections at large on their Journal, and proceed to reconsider it. If after such Reconsideration two thirds of that House shall agree to pass the Bill, it shall be sent, together with the Objections, to the other House, by which it shall likewise be reconsidered, and if approved by two thirds of that House, it shall become a Law. But in all such Cases the Votes of both Houses shall be determined by yeas and Nays, and the Names of the Persons voting for and against the Bill shall be entered on the Journal of each House respectively. If any Bill shall not be returned by the President within ten Days (Sundays excepted) after it shall have been presented to him, the Same shall be a Law, in like Manner as if he had signed it, unless the Congress by their Adjournment prevent its Return, in which Case it shall not be a Law.

Every Order, Resolution, or Vote to which the Concurrence of the Senate and House of Representatives may be necessary (except on a Question of Adjournment) shall be presented to the President of the United States; and before the Same shall take Effect, shall be approved by him, or being disapproved by him, shall be repassed by two thirds of the Senate and House of Representatives, according to the Rules and Limitations prescribed in the Case of a Bill.

Section. 8. The Congress shall have Power To lay and collect Taxes, Duties, Imposts and Excises, to pay the Debts and provide for the common Defence and general Welfare of the United States; but all Duties, Imposts and Excises shall be uniform throughout the United States;

To borrow Money on the credit of the United States;

To regulate Commerce with foreign Nations, and among the several States, and with the Indian Tribes;

To establish an uniform Rule of Naturalization, and uniform Laws on the subject of Bankruptcies throughout the United States;

To coin Money, regulate the Value thereof, and of foreign Coin, and fix the Standard of Weights and Measures;

To provide for the Punishment of counterfeiting the Securities and current Coin of the United States;

To establish Post Offices and post Roads;

To promote the Progress of Science and useful Arts, by securing for limited Times to Authors and Inventors the exclusive Right to their respective Writings and Discoveries;

To constitute Tribunals inferior to the supreme Court;

To define and punish Piracies and Felonies committed on the high Seas, and Offences against the Law of Nations;

To declare War, grant Letters of Marque and Reprisal, and make Rules concerning Captures on Land and Water;

To raise and support Armies, but no Appropriation of Money to that Use shall be for a longer Term than two Years;

To provide and maintain a Navy;

To make Rules for the Government and Regulation of the land and naval Forces;

To provide for calling forth the Militia to execute the Laws of the Union, suppress Insurrections and repel Invasions;

To provide for organizing, arming, and disciplining, the Militia, and for governing such Part of them as may be employed in the Service of the United States, reserving to the States respectively, the Appointment of the Officers, and the Authority of training the Militia according to the discipline prescribed by Congress;

To exercise exclusive Legislation in all Cases whatsoever, over such District (not exceeding ten Miles square) as may, by Cession of particular States, and the Acceptance of Congress, become the Seat of the Government of the United States, and to exercise like Authority over all Places purchased by the Consent of the Legislature of the State in which the Same shall be, for the Erection of Forts, Magazines, Arsenals, dock-Yards, and other needful Buildings;— And

To make all Laws which shall be necessary and proper for carrying into Execution the foregoing Powers, and all other Powers vested by this Constitution in the Government of the United States, or in any Department or Officer thereof.

Section. 9. The Migration or Importation of such Persons as any of the States now existing shall think proper to admit, shall not be prohibited by the Congress prior to the Year one thousand eight hundred and eight, but a Tax or duty may be imposed on such Importation, not exceeding ten dollars for each Person.

The Privilege of the Writ of Habeas Corpus shall not be suspended, unless when in Cases of Rebellion or Invasion the public Safety may require it.

No Bill of Attainder or ex post facto Law shall be passed.

No Capitation, or other direct, Tax shall be laid, unless in Proportion to the Census or Enumeration herein before directed to be taken.

No Tax or Duty shall be laid on Articles exported from any State.

No Preference shall be given by any Regulation of Commerce or Revenue to the Ports of one State over those of another: nor shall Vessels bound to, or from, one State, be obliged to enter, clear, or pay Duties in another.

No Money shall be drawn from the Treasury, but in Consequence of Appropriations made by Law; and a regular Statement and Account of the Receipts and Expenditures of all public Money shall be published from time to time.

No Title of Nobility shall be granted by the United States: And no Person holding any Office of Profit or Trust under them, shall, without the Consent of the Congress, accept of any present, Emolument, Office, or Title, of any kind whatever, from any King, Prince, or foreign State.

Section. 10. No State shall enter into any Treaty, Alliance, or Confederation; grant Letters of Marque and Reprisal; coin Money; emit Bills of Credit; make any Thing but gold and silver Coin a Tender in Payment of Debts; pass any Bill of Attainder, ex post facto Law, or Law impairing the Obligation of Contracts, or grant any Title of Nobility.

No State shall, without the Consent of the Congress, lay any Imposts or Duties on Imports or Exports, except what may be absolutely necessary for executing its inspection Laws: and the net Produce of all Duties and Imposts, laid by any State on Imports or Exports, shall be for the Use of the Treasury of the United States; and all such Laws shall be subject to the Revision and Controul of the Congress.

No State shall, without the Consent of Congress, lay any Duty of Tonnage, keep Troops, or Ships of War in time of Peace, enter into any Agreement or Compact with another State, or with a foreign Power, or engage in War, unless actually invaded, or in such imminent Danger as will not admit of delay.

Article. II.

Section. 1. The executive Power shall be vested in a President of the United States of America. He shall hold his Office during the Term of four Years, and, together with the Vice President, chosen for the same Term, be elected, as follows:

Each State shall appoint, in such Manner as the Legislature thereof may direct, a Number of Electors, equal to the whole Number of Senators and Representatives to which the State may be entitled in the Congress: but no Senator or Representative, or Person holding an Office of Trust or Profit under the United States, shall be appointed an Elector.

The Electors shall meet in their respective States, and vote by Ballot for two Persons, of whom one at least shall not be an Inhabitant of the same State with the same State with themselves. And they shall make a List of all the Persons voted for, and of the Number of Votes for each; which List they shall sign and certify, and transmit sealed to the Seat of the Government of the United States, directed to the President of the Senate. The President of the Senate shall in the Presence of the Senate and House of Representatives, open all the Certificates, and the Votes shall then be counted. The Person having the greatest Number of Votes shall be the President, if such Number be a Majority of the whole Number of Electors appointed; and if there be more than one who have such Majority, and have an equal Number of Votes, then the House of Representatives shall immediately chuse by Ballot one of them for President; and if no Person have a Majority, then from the five highest on the List the said House shall in like Manner chuse the President. But in chusing the President, the Votes shall be taken by States, the Representation from each State having one Vote; A quorum for this Purpose shall consist of a Member or Members from two thirds of the States, and a Majority of all the States shall be necessary to a Choice. In every Case, after the Choice of the President, the Person having the greatest Number of Votes of the Electors shall be the Vice President. But if there should remain two or more who have equal Votes, the Senate shall chuse from them by Ballot the Vice President.

The Congress may determine the Time of chusing the Electors, and the Day on which they shall give their Votes; which Day shall be the same throughout the United States.

No Person except a natural born Citizen, or a Citizen of the United States, at the time of the Adoption of this Constitution, shall be eligible to the Office of President; neither shall any Person be eligible to that Office who shall not have attained to the Age of thirty five Years, and been fourteen Years a Resident within the United States.

In Case of the Removal of the President from Office, or of his Death, Resignation, or Inability to discharge the Powers and Duties of the said Office, the Same shall devolve on the Vice President, and the Congress may by Law provide for the Case of Removal, Death, Resignation or Inability, both of the President and Vice President, declaring what Officer shall then act as President, and such Officer shall act accordingly, until the Disability be removed, or a President shall be elected.

The President shall, at stated Times, receive for his Services, a Compensation, which shall neither be encreased nor diminished during the Period for which he shall have been elected, and he shall not receive within that Period any other Emolument from the United States, or any of them.

Before he enter on the Execution of his Office, he shall take the following Oath or Affirmation:— "I do solemnly swear (or affirm) that I will faithfully execute the Office of President of the United States, and will to the best of my Ability, preserve, protect and defend the Constitution of the United States."

Section. 2. The President shall be Commander in Chief of the Army and Navy of the United States, and of the Militia of the several States, when called into the actual Service of the United States; he may require the Opinion, in writing, of the principal Officer in each of the executive Departments, upon any Subject relating to the Duties of their respective Offices, and he shall have Power to grant Reprieves and Pardons for Offences against the United States, except in Cases of Impeachment.

He shall have Power, by and with the Advice and Consent of the Senate, to make Treaties, provided two thirds of the Senators present concur; and he shall nominate, and by and with the Advice and Consent of the Senate, shall appoint Ambassadors, other public Ministers and Consuls, Judges of the supreme Court, and all other Officers of the United States, whose Appointments are not herein otherwise provided for, and which shall be established by Law: but the Congress may by Law vest the Appointment of such inferior Officers, as they think proper, in the President alone, in the Courts of Law, or in the Heads of Departments.

The President shall have Power to fill up all Vacancies that may happen during the Recess of the Senate, by granting Commissions which shall expire at the End of their next Session.

Section. 3. He shall from time to time give to the Congress Information of the State of the Union, and recommend to their Consideration such Measures as he shall judge necessary and expedient; he may, on extraordinary Occasions, convene both Houses, or either of them, and in Case of Disagreement between them, with Respect to the Time of Adjournment, he may adjourn them to such Time as he shall think proper; he shall receive Ambassadors and other public Ministers; he shall take Care that the Laws be faithfully executed, and shall Commission all the Officers of the United States.

Section. 4. The President, Vice President and all civil Officers of the United States, shall be removed from Office on Impeachment for, and Conviction of, Treason, Bribery, or other high Crimes and Misdemeanors.

Article III.

Section. 1. The judicial Power of the United States, shall be vested in one supreme Court, and in such inferior Courts as the Congress may from time to time ordain and establish. The Judges, both of the supreme and inferior Courts, shall hold their Offices during good Behaviour, and shall, at stated Times, receive for their Services, a Compensation, which shall not be diminished during their Continuance in Office.

Section. 2. The judicial Power shall extend to all Cases, in Law and Equity, arising under this Constitution, the Laws of the United States, and Treaties made, or which shall be made, under their Authority;— to all Cases affecting Ambassadors, other public Ministers and Consuls;— to all Cases of admiralty and maritime Jurisdiction;— to Controversies to which the United States shall be a Party;— to Controversies between two or more States;— between a State and Citizens of another State,— between Citizens of different States,— between Citizens of the same State claiming Lands under Grants of different States, and between a State, or the Citizens thereof, and foreign States, Citizens or Subjects.

In all Cases affecting Ambassadors, other public Ministers and Consuls, and those in which a State shall be Party, the supreme Court shall have original Jurisdiction. In all the other Cases before mentioned, the supreme Court shall have appellate Jurisdiction, both as to Law and Fact, with such Exceptions, and under such Regulations as the Congress shall make.

The Trial of all Crimes, except in Cases of Impeachment, shall be by Jury; and such Trial shall be held in the State where the said Crimes shall have been committed; but when not committed within any State, the Trial shall be at such Place or Places as the Congress may by Law have directed.

Section. 3. Treason against the United States, shall consist only in levying War against them, or in adhering to their Enemies, giving them Aid and Comfort. No Person shall be convicted of Treason unless on the Testimony of two Witnesses to the same overt Act, or on Confession in open Court.

The Congress shall have Power to declare the Punishment of Treason, but no Attainder of Treason shall work Corruption of Blood, or Forfeiture except during the Life of the Person attainted.

Article. IV.

Section. 1. Full Faith and Credit shall be given in each State to the public Acts, Records, and judicial Proceedings of every other State. And the

Congress may by general Laws prescribe the Manner in which such Acts, Records and Proceedings shall be proved, and the Effect thereof.

Section. 2. The Citizens of each State shall be entitled to all Privileges and Immunities of Citizens in the several States.

A Person charged in any State with Treason, Felony, or other Crime, who shall flee from Justice, and be found in another State, shall on Demand of the executive Authority of the State from which he fled, be delivered up, to be removed to the State having Jurisdiction of the Crime.

No Person held to Service or Labour in one State, under the Laws thereof, escaping into another, shall in Consequence of any Law or Regulation therein, be discharged from such Service or Labour, but shall be delivered up on Claim of the Party to whom such Service or Labour may be due.

Section. 3. New States may be admitted by the Congress into this Union; but no new State shall be formed or erected within the Jurisdiction of any other State; nor any State be formed by the Junction of two or more States, or Parts of States, without the Consent of the Legislatures of the States concerned as well as of the Congress.

The Congress shall have Power to dispose of and make all needful Rules and Regulations respecting the Territory or other Property belonging to the United States; and nothing in this Constitution shall be so construed as to Prejudice any Claims of the United States, or of any particular State.

Section. 4. The United States shall guarantee to every State in this Union a Republican Form of Government, and shall protect each of them against Invasion; and on Application of the Legislature, or of the Executive (when the Legislature cannot be convened) against domestic Violence.

Article. V.

The Congress, whenever two thirds of both Houses shall deem it necessary, shall propose Amendments to this Constitution, or, on the Application of the Legislatures of two thirds of the several States, shall call a Convention for proposing Amendments, which, in either Case, shall be valid to all Intents and Purposes, as Part of this Constitution, when ratified by the Legislatures of three fourths of the several States, or by Conventions in three fourths thereof, as the one or the other Mode of Ratification may be proposed by the Congress; Provided that no Amendment which may be made prior to the Year one thousand eight hundred and eight shall in any Manner affect the first and fourth Clauses in the Ninth Section of the first Article; and that no State, without its Consent, shall be deprived of its equal Suffrage in the Senate.

Article. VI.

All Debts contracted and Engagements entered into, before the Adoption of this Constitution, shall be as valid against the United States under this Constitution, as under the Confederation.

This Constitution, and the Laws of the United States which shall be made in Pursuance thereof; and all Treaties made, or which shall be made, under the Authority of the United States, shall be the supreme Law of the Land; and the Judges in every State shall be bound thereby, any Thing in the Constitution or Laws of any State to the Contrary notwithstanding.

The Senators and Representatives before mentioned, and the Members of the several State Legislatures, and all executive and judicial Officers, both of the United States and of the several States, shall be bound by Oath or Affirmation, to support this Constitution; but no religious Test shall ever be required as a Qualification to any Office or public Trust under the United States.

Article. VII.

The Ratification of the Conventions of nine States, shall be sufficient for the Establishment of this Constitution between the States so ratifying the Same.

The Word, "the," being interlined between the seventh and eighth Lines of the first Page, The Word "Thirty" being partly written on an Erazure in the fifteenth Line of the first Page. The Words "is tried" being interlined between the thirty second and thirty third Lines of the first Page and the Word "the" being interlined between the forty third and forty fourth Lines of the second Page.

Attest William Jackson Secretary

done in Convention by the Unanimous Consent of the States present the Seventeenth Day of September in the Year of our Lord one thousand seven hundred and Eighty seven and of the Independance of the United States of America the Twelfth In Witness whereof We have hereunto subscribed our Names,

G°. Washington—Presid.t and deputy from Virginia

Delaware { Geo: Read
Gunning Bedford jun
John Dickinson
Richard Bassett
Jaco: Broom

Maryland { James McHenry
Dan of St Thos. Jenifer
Danl Carroll

Virginia { John Blair—
James Madison Jr.

North Carolina { Wm. Blount
Richd. Dobbs Spaight.
Hu Williamson

South Carolina { J. Rutledge
Charles Cotesworth Pinckney
Charles Pinckney
Pierce Butler

Georgia { William Few

New Hampshire { John Langdon
Nicholas Gilman

Massachusetts { Nathaniel Gorham
Rufus King

Connecticut { Wm. Saml. Johnson
Roger Sherman

New York . . Alexander Hamilton

New Jersey { Wil: Livingston
David Brearley
Wm. Paterson
Jona: Dayton

Pennsylvania { B Franklin
Thomas Mifflin
Robt. Morris
Geo. Clymer
Thos. FitzSimons
Jared Ingersoll
James Wilson
Gouv Morris

Bill of Rights, ratified December 15, 1791

The document on permanent display is the Joint Resolution passed by Congress on September 25, 1789, proposing twelve—not ten—amendments. The first article listed, concerning the ratio of constituents to each congressional representative, was never ratified by the states; the second article listed, concerning congressional pay, was ratified in 1992 as the Twenty-seventh Amendment.

The Bill of Rights was engrossed by William Lambert, a congressional clerk, and was signed by Frederick Augustus Muhlenberg, Speaker of the House, on September 28, 1789, and by John Adams, President of the Senate, shortly thereafter. *National Archives, General Records of the U.S. Government*

Congress OF THE United States,

begun and held at the City of New-York, on
Wednesday the fourth of March, one thousand seven hundred and eighty-nine.

THE Conventions of a number of the States, having at the time of their adopting the Constitution, expressed a desire, in order to prevent misconstruction or abuse of its powers, that further declaratory and restrictive clauses should be added: And as extending the ground of public confidence in the Government, will best ensure the beneficent ends of its institution.

RESOLVED by the Senate and House of Representatives of the United States of America, in Congress assembled, two thirds of both Houses concurring, that the following Articles be proposed to the Legislatures of the several States, as amendments to the Constitution of the United States, all, or any of which Articles, when ratified by three fourths of the said Legislatures, to be valid to all intents and purposes, as part of the said Constitution; viz.

ARTICLES in addition to, and Amendment of the Constitution of the United States of America, proposed by Congress, and ratified by the Legislatures of the several States, pursuant to the fifth Article of the original Constitution.

Article the first.... After the first enumeration required by the first Article of the Constitution, there shall be one Representative for every thirty thousand, until the number shall amount to one hundred, after which, the proportion shall be so regulated by Congress, that there shall be not less than one hundred Representatives, nor less than one Representative for every forty thousand persons, until the number of Representatives shall amount to two hundred; after which the proportion shall be so regulated by Congress, that there shall not be less than two hundred Representatives, nor more than one Representative for every fifty thousand persons.

Article the second.... No law, varying the compensation for the services of the Senators and Representatives, shall take effect, until an election of Representatives shall have intervened.

Article the third.... Congress shall make no law respecting an establishment of religion, or prohibiting the free exercise thereof; or abridging the freedom of speech, or of the press; or the right of the people peaceably to assemble, and to petition the Government for a redress of grievances.

Article the fourth.... A well regulated militia, being necessary to the security of a free State, the right of the people to keep and bear arms, shall not be infringed.

Article the fifth.... No soldier shall, in time of peace be quartered in any house, without the consent of the owner, nor in time of war, but in a manner to be prescribed by law.

Article the sixth.... The right of the people to be secure in their persons, houses, papers, and effects, against unreasonable searches and seizures, shall not be violated, and no warrants shall issue, but upon probable cause, supported by oath or affirmation, and particularly describing the place to be searched, and the persons or things to be seized.

Article the seventh.... No person shall be held to answer for a capital, or otherwise infamous crime, unless on a presentment or indictment of a Grand Jury, except in cases arising in the land or naval forces, or in the Militia, when in actual service in time of War or public danger; nor shall any person be subject for the same offence to be twice put in jeopardy of life or limb; nor shall be compelled in any criminal case to be a witness against himself, nor be deprived of life, liberty, or property, without due process of law; nor shall private property be taken for public use, without just compensation.

Article the eighth.... In all criminal prosecutions, the accused shall enjoy the right to a speedy and public trial, by an impartial jury of the State and district wherein the crime shall have been committed, which district shall have been previously ascertained by law, and to be informed of the nature and cause of the accusation; to be confronted with the witnesses against him; to have compulsory process for obtaining witnesses in his favor, and to have the Assistance of Counsel for his defence.

Article the ninth.... In suits at common law, where the value in controversy shall exceed twenty dollars, the right of trial by jury shall be preserved, and no fact tried by a jury, shall be otherwise re-examined in any Court of the United States, than according to the rules of the common law.

Article the tenth.... Excessive bail shall not be required, nor excessive fines imposed, nor cruel and unusual punishments inflicted.

Article the eleventh.... The enumeration in the Constitution, of certain rights, shall not be construed to deny or disparage others retained by the people.

Article the twelfth.... The powers not delegated to the United States by the Constitution, nor prohibited by it to the States, are reserved to the States respectively, or to the people.

ATTEST,

Frederick Augustus Muhlenberg, Speaker of the House of Representatives.

John Adams, Vice President of the United States, and President of the Senate.

John Beckley, Clerk of the House of Representatives.
Sam. A. Otis, Secretary of the Senate.

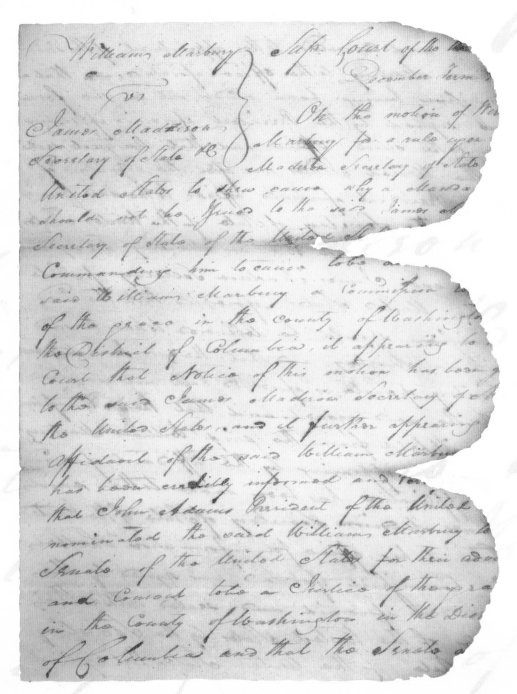

Order served on Secretary of State James Madison by the U.S. Supreme Court, March 22, 1802

In March 1801, in the final days of his administration, President John Adams appointed William Marbury as Justice of the Peace in the District of Columbia, but Secretary of State John Marshall failed to deliver it. When incoming Secretary of State James Madison refused to deliver Marbury's commission, Marbury sued to obtain it. He asked the Supreme Court to order Madison to deliver the commission.

John Marshall, who became Chief Justice of the Supreme Court in 1801, wrote the landmark decision. The Court's opinion declared the law that authorized the Supreme Court to act on Marbury's behalf to be unconstitutional. Never before had the Supreme Court exercised its authority to declare an act of Congress to be unconstitutional. With this ruling on an apparently trivial matter, Marshall set the course for the judiciary to be a coequal branch of government.

This document bears the marks of the Capitol fire of 1898.
National Archives, Records of the Supreme Court of the United States

Marbury v. *Madison*, 1803

Although most of the Framers of the Constitution anticipated that the Federal judiciary would be the weakest branch of Government, the U.S. Supreme Court has come to wield enormous power with decisions that have reached into the lives of every citizen and resolved some of the most dramatic confrontations in U.S. history. The word of the Supreme Court is final. Overturning its decisions often requires an amendment to the Constitution or a revision of Federal law.

The power of the Supreme Court has evolved over time, through a series of milestone court cases. One of the Court's most fundamental powers is judicial review—the power to judge the constitutionality of any act or law of the executive or legislative branch. Some of

John Marshall, oil painting by Rembrandt Peale, 1826

During the thirty-five years that John Marshall served as Chief Justice of the U.S. Supreme Court, he asserted both the power of the judiciary as a coequal branch of Government and the supremacy of Federal authority.
Courtesy of the Supreme Court of the United States, Washington, DC

"The people made the Constitution, and the people can unmake it. It is the creature of their will, and lives only by their will."

Chief Justice John Marshall, 1821

the Framers expected the Supreme Court to take on the role of determining the constitutionality of Congress's laws, but the Constitution did not explicitly assign it to the Court. *Marbury* v. *Madison*, the 1803 landmark Supreme Court case, established the power of judicial review. From the modest claim of William Marbury, who sought a low-paying appointment as a District of Columbia Justice of the Peace, emerged a Supreme Court decision that established one of the cornerstones of the American constitutional system.

"Let the Land rejoice,
for you have bought Louisiana
for a Song."

Gen. Horatio Gates to President Thomas Jefferson,
July 18, 1803

Map No. 4.

Territory of Louisiana ceded by France to the
United States by the Treaty of April 30, 1803,
reprinted from the pamphlet "Historical
Sketch of Louisiana," published by the General
Land Office, 1933

National Archives, Records of the Bureau of
Land Management

WESTWARD EXPANSION
THE LOUISIANA PURCHASE

In 1803, with one bold move, President Thomas Jefferson's administration doubled the size of the United States. France's offer of the Louisiana Territory—828,000 square miles of land extending west of the Mississippi River, in exchange for $15 million—was simply too good to resist. The Treaty, dated April 30, 1803, was signed in Paris by Robert Livingston and James Monroe and ratified by Congress on October 20. Fifteen states or parts of states were carved from the vast territory, which was the single largest acquisition of land in U.S. history.

Sixteen years earlier, critics of the Constitution had argued that the original thirteen states already covered too vast a territory to be under a single government. In 1803, some European powers predicted that the huge addition of land would be the death knell of the American experiment and would cause the Union to degenerate into competing and warring factions. Jefferson, however, believed it would provide "a wide-spread field for the blessings of freedom." The Louisiana Territory added to the United States a wealth of natural resources beyond anyone's calculations. Westward expansion was a disaster for the many indigenous peoples who had no say in the sale of lands they had inhabited for generations. But the Louisiana Purchase did not weaken the Union; it strengthened it. The transaction was more than a brilliant act of diplomacy or a shrewd real estate deal. It was a vote of confidence in the future of a fledgling nation.

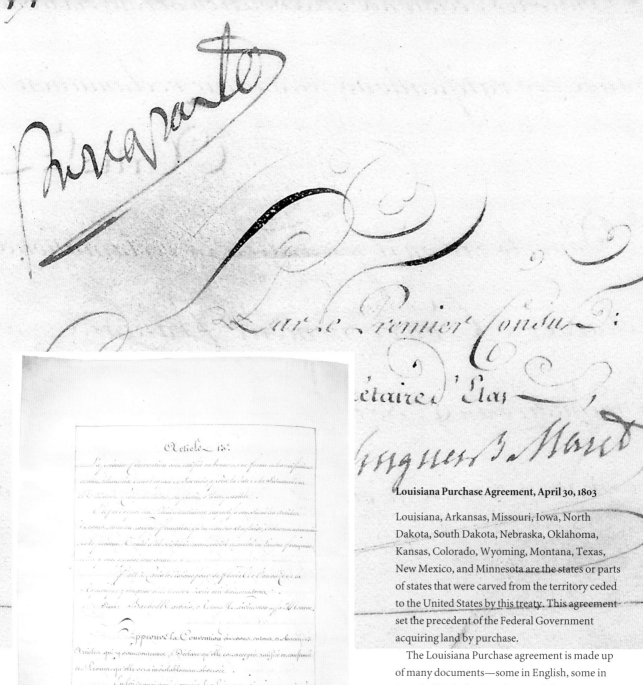

Louisiana Purchase Agreement, April 30, 1803

Louisiana, Arkansas, Missouri, Iowa, North Dakota, South Dakota, Nebraska, Oklahoma, Kansas, Colorado, Wyoming, Montana, Texas, New Mexico, and Minnesota are the states or parts of states that were carved from the territory ceded to the United States by this treaty. This agreement set the precedent of the Federal Government acquiring land by purchase.

The Louisiana Purchase agreement is made up of many documents—some in English, some in French. This is the French copy of the agreement ceding the territory to the United States. The initials "P.F.," embroidered on the front and back covers, stand for "Peuple Français," which translated means "French People." With a flourish, Napoleon, First Consul of the French Republic, signed his name "Bonaparte" on the final page of the document and thus created a vast nation that could stand against Great Britain.

National Archives, General Records of the U.S. Government

The Bitterroot Range of the Rocky Mountains, from the Montana–Idaho border, photograph by Sam Abell

Sam Abell/National Geographic Image Collection

Above:

**"Confederate dead behind stone wall,"
photograph from the Mathew Brady
Collection, May 1863**

*National Archives, Records of the
Office of the Chief Signal Officer*

Right:

**Ruins of Arsenal, Richmond, Virginia,
April 1865**

*National Archives, Records of the War
Department General and Special
Staffs*

*Alex Gardner, photographer
April 1865*

THE CIVIL WAR
THE UNION SEALED IN BLOOD

September 17, 1862, the 75th anniversary of the signing of the Constitution, was the bloodiest single day in U.S. history. An estimated 6,300 Americans—Union and Confederate soldiers—died that day at Antietam, Maryland, in a savage battle that took place nearly a year and a half into the Civil War. It was one day in a war that raged from 1861–65 and cost some 623,000 lives. In a total national population of twenty-seven million in 1860, that number would be proportionately equivalent to losing more than five million today.

> *"The fiery trial through which we pass, will light us down, in honor or dishonor, to the latest generation.... In giving freedom to the slave, we assure freedom to the free—honorable alike in what we give, and what we preserve. We shall nobly save, or meanly lose, the last best, hope of earth."*

President Abraham Lincoln, December 1, 1862

At stake in the Civil War was the survival of the United States of America as a single nation. Eleven Southern states, invoking the spirit of 1776, seceded from the Union in 1861 to form a nation they named the Confederate States of America. The Federal Government refused to allow it. Massive armies representing the Union and the Confederacy squared off in a conflict that tested the experiment in self-government as never before. At the end of the Civil War's carnage, the primacy of the Federal Government over the states was indisputably upheld.

Americans had been wrestling with this fundamental question of nationhood since the earliest days of the Revolution. In 1774, as the British colonists struggled to unite in the cause of American liberty, Patrick Henry rose to address the Continental Congress in one of its earliest sessions: "The distinctions between Virginians, Pennsylvanians and New Englanders are no more. I am not a Virginian, but an American." It took the Civil War to make it so.

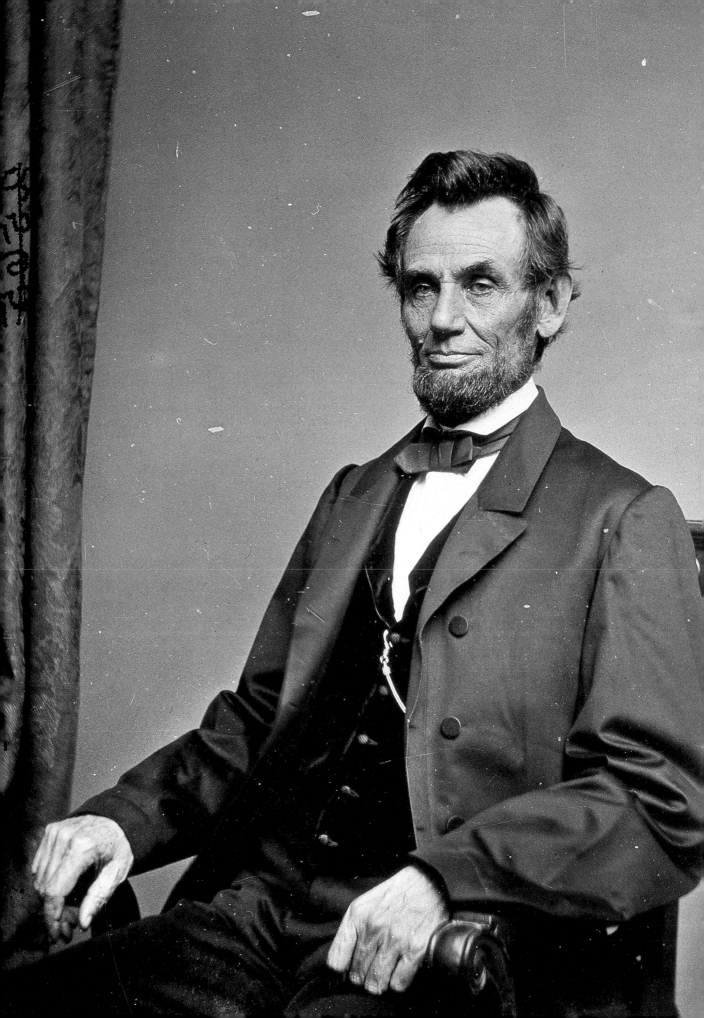

Opposite page:

Abraham Lincoln, photograph from the Mathew Brady Collection, ca. 1860–65

In his first inaugural address in 1861, President Abraham Lincoln asserted that secession was unconstitutional—that the Union of the states was perpetual, and states could not leave it at will.

National Archives, Records of the Office of the Chief Signal Officer

President Abraham Lincoln's Message to Congress on the State of the Union, December 1, 1862, selected pages

The Constitution requires that the President "shall from time to time give to the Congress Information of the State of the Union." As was the custom in the nineteenth century, the President delivered his message in writing; a congressional clerk read it aloud. Here is the final portion of President Lincoln's State of the Union message to Congress for 1862.

As the Union lay in shambles, the shining vision of the nation's Founders persisted in the mind of President Lincoln. In the conclusion, the best remembered portion of this message, Lincoln referred to the United States as "the last best, hope of earth."

National Archives, Records of the U.S. Senate, reproduced with the permission of the U.S. Senate

By the President of the United States of America:

A Proclamation.

Whereas, on the twenty-second day of September, in the year of our Lord one thousand eight hundred and sixty-two, a proclamation was issued by the President of the United States, containing, among other things, the following, to wit:

"That on the first day of January, in the year of our Lord one thousand eight hundred and sixty-three, all persons held as slaves within "any State or designated part of a State, the people "whereof shall then be in rebellion against the "United States, shall be then, thenceforward, and "forever free; and the Executive Government of the "United States, including the military and naval "authority thereof, will recognize and maintain "the freedom of such persons, and will do no "act or acts to repress such persons, or any of them, "in any efforts they may make for their actual "freedom.

"That the Executive will

one thousand eight hundred and sixty three, and of the Independence of the United States of America the eighty-seventh.

Abraham Lincoln

By the President:
William H. Seward
Secretary of State

THE END OF SLAVERY IN THE UNITED STATES
THE EMANCIPATION PROCLAMATION AND THE
THIRTEENTH AMENDMENT

The four years of Civil War that ripped apart the nation from 1861–65 achieved what seventy-five years of compromise could not: it resolved once and for all the question of slavery in the United States. By 1860, there were four and a half million slaves in the United States. Military necessity and the force of human passion for liberty pushed emancipation to the top of the nation's agenda. Two major milestones marked slavery's final destruction during the war years: the Emancipation Proclamation and the Thirteenth Amendment to the Constitution.

Opposite page:
The Emancipation Proclamation, January 1, 1863

When Abraham Lincoln signed the Emancipation Proclamation on January 1, 1863, he said, "I never in my life, felt more certain that I was doing right than I do in signing this paper." In this document, President Lincoln declared that "all persons held as slaves" within the rebellious areas "are and henceforward shall be free."

Despite that expansive wording, the Emancipation Proclamation was limited in many ways. It applied only to states that had seceded from the Union, leaving slavery untouched in the loyal border states. It expressly exempted parts of the Confederacy that had already come under Northern control. Most important, the freedom it promised depended upon Union military victory.

While the Emancipation Proclamation did not end slavery in the nation, it fundamentally trans-formed the character of the war. After January 1, 1863, every advance of Federal troops expanded the domain of freedom. Moreover, the liberated themselves became liberators, for the Proclamation announced the acceptance of black men into the Union army and navy. By the end of the war, nearly 200,000 black soldiers and sailors had fought for the Union and freedom.

The Emancipation Proclamation added moral force to the Union cause and strengthened the Union both militarily and politically. As a mile-stone along the road to slavery's final destruction, the Emancipation Proclamation has assumed a place among the great documents of human freedom.
National Archives, General Records of the U.S. Government

"Watch Meeting—Dec. 31st, 1862—Waiting for the
Hour," slaves awaiting the moment when the
Emancipation Proclamation takes effect, oil paint-
ing by William Tolman Carlton, 1863

The Emancipation Proclamation captured the
imagination of millions of Americans and trans-
formed the Civil War from a war for union into
a crusade for freedom.

The original of this painting hangs in the
White House, in the room where President Lincoln
signed the Emancipation Proclamation on
January 1, 1863.
*Courtesy of The White House Historical
Association (White House Collection),
Washington, DC*

House of Representatives of the
United States of America in
Congress assembled, (two thirds
of both Houses concurring,)
That the following article be
proposed to the legislatures
of the several states as an
amendment to the constitution
of the United States, which,
when ratified by three fourths
of said legislatures, shall be
valid, to all intents and purposes, as a part of the said constitution, namely:—
"Article XIII.
"Section 1. Neither slavery
nor involuntary servitude, except as a punishment for crime
whereof the party shall have

**Proclamation of the Secretary of State announcing
the ratification of the Thirteenth Amendment to
the Constitution, December 18, 1865, selected pages**

President Lincoln feared that the Emancipation
Proclamation would be overturned once the war
ended. A constitutional amendment would ensure
that slavery could never again resurface. Congress
formally proposed the Thirteenth Amendment
outlawing slavery on January 31, 1865; it was ratified on December 6, 1865.

In less than fifty words, the Thirteenth
Amendment outlawed slavery in the United States.
*National Archives, General Records of the U.S.
Government*

uly convicted, shall exist
in the United States, or
place subject to their juris-
...
...ction 2. Congress shall
power to enforce this ar-
by appropriate legislation."

nd, whereas it appears,
official documents on
this Department, that
the amendment to the Constitution of the United States
proposed, as aforesaid, has
been ratified by the legislatures
of the States of Illinois, Rhode
Island, Michigan, Maryland,
New York, West Virginia, Maine,
Kansas, Massachusetts, Pennsylvania,

"The bosom of America is open to receive not only the Opulent & respectable Stranger, but the oppressed & persecuted of all Nations & Religions; whom we shall wellcome to a participation of all our rights & previleges."

George Washington, Address to Irish Immigrants,
draft handwritten by David Humphries, December 2, 1783

America's earliest settlers who came in search of religious freedom in the seventeenth century passed on a vision of America as a beacon of hope to the world that still shines brightly today. Between 1820 and 2001, more than sixty-seven million people came to the United States from every corner of the globe, lured by the promise of liberty and opportunity. The open-door policies of the early years of the Republic eventually gave way in the late nineteenth century to more restrictive measures driven by concerns for the nation's economy and security. Fear of foreigners and racial prejudice have also influenced policies that excluded rather than welcomed immigrants. But the wish to honor the ideal of America as a safe haven persists. Two-thirds of the seventy million people who have left Europe since 1600 have come to America. Millions more have come from Asia, Africa, and Latin America.

Today, the United States pulses with the energy of a dizzying mix of cultures, races, religions, and languages. The people of the United States are joined together, not by religion, race, or genealogy, but by a shared set of beliefs about freedom. In 1989, the fortieth President of the United States, Ronald Reagan, reflected on the current state of the American Dream: "After 200 years . . . [America's] still a beacon, still a magnet for all who must have freedom, for all the pilgrims from all the lost places who are hurtling through the darkness, toward home."

Opposite page:
Deed of Gift, Statue of Liberty, July 4, 1884

"Liberty Enlightening the World," more commonly known as the Statue of Liberty, was a gift from the people of France to the people of the United States. It stands in New York Harbor. Conceived by the French sculptor Frédéric de Bartholdi, it celebrates a century of friendship between the two nations. In her left arm, Lady Liberty holds a tablet inscribed with the date of the Declaration of Independence, July 4, 1776.

Built on a colossal scale, the statue has become one of the most potent symbols of human freedom. The famous sonnet, composed by Emma Lazarus in 1883 and inscribed on the pedestal in 1903, gives voice to a strain of idealism that celebrates the United States as a refuge for the oppressed peoples of the world:

"Give me your tired, your poor,
Your huddled masses yearning to breathe free,
The wretched refuse of your teeming shore.
Send these, the homeless tempest-tost to me,
I lift my lamp beside the golden door!"

From "The New Colossus" by Emma Lazarus

National Archives, General Records of the Department of State

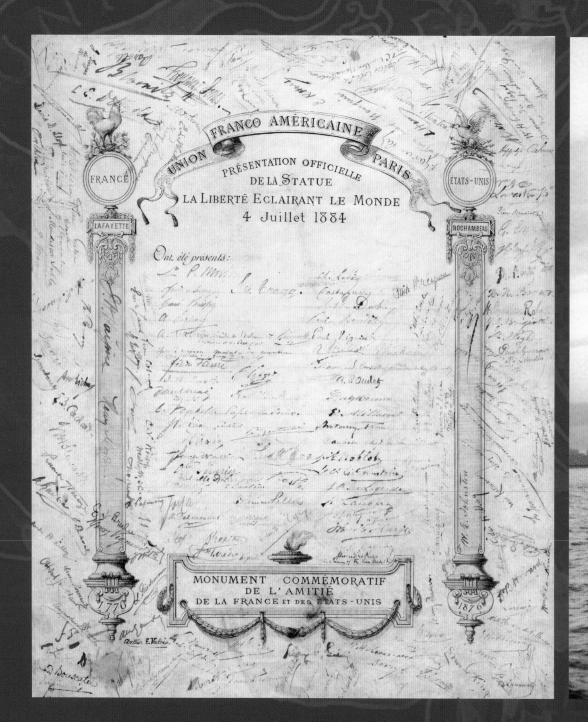

**Statue of Liberty Official Presentation Document,
July 4, 1884**

With this document, the Statue of Liberty was formally presented as a gift to the people of the United States. At a ceremony in Paris, in the foundry yard where "Lady Liberty" was constructed, Levi P. Morton, U.S. Minister to France, accepted the statue on behalf of the President and the people of the United States. The document is nearly covered by the signatures of the U.S. and French officials and dignitaries who attended the ceremony that day; Morton's is at the top of the column of signatures inside the decorative border.

National Archives, General Records of the Department of State

Statue of Liberty, ca. 1955–67

*National Archives, Records of the Social Security
Administration*

No sir. When was it? In the latter part
of October? What it was it.
(Objection. Overruled)
The Registry of Election was offered in evidence
& marked "Ex. A."
Beverly W. Jones recalled.
By Mr. Van Voorhis. Do you recollect anything
farther that was said by Mr. Warner? Yes
sir I recollect his saying my that — on ask-
ing me the question "Do you know the
penalty for not registering these names.
I told him I did.
By Mr. Pound. You have told all that you
recollect of Mr. Warner's conversation now?
Yes sir
Pltff's Case Closed

Defts Case

Susan B. Anthony sworn in her own
behalf testified:
Are you the person spoken of as defendant
Yes, sir. Previous to voting at the 1st District
poll in the 8th Ward, did you take the advice
of counsel upon voting? Yes, sir. Who was it you
talked with? Judge Henry R. Selden. What did
he advise you with reference to your legal right
to vote? He said it was the only way to find

out what the law was upon the subject—
to bring it to a test. Did he advise you
to go and offer your vote? Yes, sir. State whether
or not prior to such advice you had retained
Mr. Selden to defend in this action? No, sir,
I first went to Judge Selden to sound him if we
should want him. Have you anything further to
say upon Judge Selden's advice? I think it
was sound. Did he give you an opinion upon the subject? He was like all the rest of you
lawyers — he had not studied the question
What did he advise you? He left me with the
opinion — that he was an honest man; but
he would study it up thoroughly, & decide according
to the law. Did you have any doubt yourself of
your right to vote? Not a particle.
Cross examined:
Would you not have made the same efforts
to vote that you did do if you had not consulted with Judge Selden? Yes, sir. (I hope
the court understands that I did not con-
sult anyone untill after I had voted) Was
you not influenced by his advice in
the matter at all? No, sir. You went

EXPANSION OF RIGHTS AND LIBERTIES
THE RIGHT OF SUFFRAGE

When the Constitution took effect in 1789, it did not "secure the blessings of liberty" to all people. The expansion of rights and liberties has been achieved over time, as people once excluded from the protections of the Constitution asserted their rights set forth in the

---

"It was we, the people, not we, the white male citizens,
nor yet we, the male citizens; but we, the whole people,
who formed this Union."

Susan B. Anthony, champion of woman suffrage, 1873

Declaration of Independence. These Americans have fostered movements resulting in laws, Supreme Court decisions, and constitutional amendments that have narrowed the gap between the ideal and the reality of American freedom.

At the time of the first Presidential election in 1789, only 6 percent of the population—white, male property owners—was eligible to vote. The Fifteenth Amendment extended the right to vote to former male slaves in 1870; American Indians gained the vote under a law passed by Congress in 1924; and women gained the vote with the ratification of the Nineteenth Amendment in 1920.

Opposite page, bottom:
Susan B. Anthony, not dated

Susan B. Anthony devoted some fifty years of her life to the cause of woman suffrage. After casting her ballot in the 1872 election in her hometown of Rochester, New York, she was arrested, indicted, tried, and convicted for voting illegally. At her two-day trial in June 1873, which she described as "the greatest judicial outrage history has ever recorded," she was convicted and sentenced to pay a fine of $100 and court costs.

Women gained the vote with the passage of the Nineteenth Amendment to the Constitution in 1920, fourteen years after Anthony's death.
National Archives, Records of the Women's Bureau

Opposite page, top:
Transcript of Susan B. Anthony's testimony in a pre-trial hearing before a U.S. Commissioner, November 29, 1872, selected pages

After Anthony's arrest for "illegal voting," in the election of 1872, there was a hearing to determine if she had, in fact, broken the law. Anthony's testimony begins approximately two-thirds down the page under "Defts. [abbreviation for Defendant's] Case." When asked by her lawyer John Van Voorhis if she had any doubt of her right to vote, she replied, "not a particle."

The witnesses against Anthony at the hearing were a male complainant who witnessed the vote and the three male election inspectors who accepted her ballot.
National Archives—Northeast Region (New York City), Records of District Courts of the United States

One hundred years after the Civil War, civil rights activists were still engaged in the struggle to end racial discrimination and segregation that barred African Americans from enjoying the full rights of citizenship. In a series of dramatic confrontations throughout the South and other parts of the country, activists challenged discriminatory laws and customs. In August 1963, more than 250,000 people marched on Washington to protest racial discrimination in the nation and to voice support for civil rights legislation that would end it. Following the longest Senate debate in U.S. history, Congress passed the Civil Rights Bill on July 2, 1964; just over a year later, the Voting Rights Act was signed into law.

President Johnson speaking at the signing ceremony of the Civil Rights Act, photograph by O.J. Rapp, July 2, 1964

Signing the Civil Rights Bill into law two days before the nation celebrated the 188th anniversary of the Declaration of Independence, President Johnson harkened back to the guiding spirit of the American Revolution and to the brave patriots who founded this nation in the name of freedom.

"Americans of every race and color have died in battle to protect our freedom," he said, and he concluded his remarks that day with a plea for unity: "Let us close the springs of racial poison. Let us pray for wise and understanding hearts. Let us lay aside irrelevant differences and make our Nation whole."

National Archives, Lyndon Baines Johnson Library, Austin, Texas

H. R. 7152 PUBLIC LAW 88-352

Eighty-eighth Congress of the United States of America

AT THE SECOND SESSION

Begun and held at the City of Washington on Tuesday, the seventh day of January, one thousand nine hundred and sixty-four

An Act

To enforce the constitutional right to vote, to confer jurisdiction upon the district courts of the United States to provide injunctive relief against discrimination in public accommodations, to authorize the Attorney General to institute suits to protect constitutional rights in public facilities and public education, to extend the Commission on Civil Rights, to prevent discrimination in Federally assisted programs, to establish a Commission on Equal Employment Opportunity, and for other purposes.

Be it enacted by the Senate and House of Representatives of the United States of America in Congress assembled, That this Act may be cited as the "Civil Rights Act of 1964".

TITLE I—VOTING RIGHTS

Sec. 101. Section 2004 of the Revised Statutes (42 U.S.C. 1971), as amended by section 131 of the Civil Rights Act of 1957 (71 Stat. 637), and as further amended by section 601 of the Civil Rights Act of 1960 (74 Stat. 90), is further amended as follows:

(a) Insert "1" after "(a)" in subsection (a) and add at the end of subsection (a) the following new paragraphs:

"(2) No person acting under color of law shall—

"(A) in determining whether any individual is qualified under State law or laws to vote in any Federal election, apply any standard, practice, or procedure different from the standards, practices, or procedures applied under such law or laws to other individuals within the same county, parish, or similar political subdivision who have been found by State officials to be qualified to vote;

"(B) deny the right of any individual to vote in any Federal election because of an error or omission on any record or paper relating to any application, registration, or other act requisite to voting, if such error or omission is not material in determining whether such individual is qualified under State law to vote in such election; or

"(C) employ any literacy test as a qualification for voting in any Federal election unless (i) such test is administered to each individual and is conducted wholly in writing, and (ii) a certified copy of the test and of the answers given by the individual is furnished to him within twenty-five days of the submission of his request made within the period of time during which records and papers are required to be retained and preserved pursuant to title III of the Civil Rights Act of 1960 (42 U.S.C. 1974-74e; 74 Stat. 88): *Provided, however,* That the Attorney General may enter into agreements with appropriate State or local authorities that preparation, conduct, and maintenance of such tests in accordance with the provisions of applicable State or local law, including such special provisions as are necessary in the preparation, conduct, and maintenance of such tests for persons who are blind or otherwise physically handicapped, meet the purposes of this subparagraph and constitute compliance therewith.

"(3) For purposes of this subsection—

"(A) the term 'vote' shall have the same meaning as in subsection (e) of this section;

"(B) the phrase 'literacy test' includes any test of the ability to read, write, understand, or interpret any matter."

(b) Insert immediately following the period at the end of the first sentence of subsection (c) the following new sentence: "If in any such proceeding literacy is a relevant fact there shall be a rebuttable

> *"We have talked long enough in this country about equal rights. We have talked for one hundred years or more. It is time now to write the next chapter, and to write it in the books of law."*
>
> President Lyndon Johnson, November 27, 1963

Civil Rights Act, July 2, 1964, page 1

This law is the most sweeping civil rights legislation since Reconstruction. It bans racial discrimination in privately owned accommodations for the public, such as restaurants, stores, gas stations, and hotels; it authorizes the Attorney General to ban racial segregation in public schools, hospitals, parks, libraries, and museums. It threatens Federally funded institutions with the loss of Federal funds if they continue to discriminate. And it prohibits discrimination in hiring practices.

National Archives, General Records of the U.S. Government

President Lyndon B. Johnson hands a souvenir pen to Rev. Martin Luther King, Jr., after the ceremony marking the signing of the Voting Rights Act, August 6, 1965

Before the Voting Rights Act went into effect, only some 23 percent of voting-age blacks were registered in the United States; by 1969, that number had increased to 61 percent.

National Archives, Records of the U.S. Information Agency

THERE IS ONE SIGN THE SOVIETS CAN MAKE THAT
WOULD BE UNMISTAKABLE./THAT WOULD ADVANCE
DRAMATICALLY THE CAUSE OF FREEDOM AND PEACE.
    GENERAL SECRETARY GORBACHEV, IF YOU
SEEK PEACE /- IF YOU SEEK PROSPERITY FOR
THE SOVIET UNION AND EASTERN EUROPE /-
IF YOU SEEK LIBERALIZATION: COME HERE,
TO THIS GATE.
    MR. GORBACHEV, OPEN THIS GATE.
    MR. GORBACHEV, TEAR DOWN THIS WALL.
    I UNDERSTAND THE FEAR OF WAR AND THE
PAIN OF DIVISION THAT AFFLICT THIS
CONTINENT /- AND I PLEDGE TO YOU MY
COUNTRY's EFFORTS TO HELP OVERCOME THESE
BURDENS. TO BE SURE, WE IN THE WEST MUST
RESIST SOVIET EXPANSION. SO WE MUST
MAINTAIN DEFENSES OF UNASSAILABLE STRENGTH.
YET WE SEEK PEACE. SO WE MUST STRIVE TO
REDUCE ARMS ON BOTH SIDES.

Speech card from President Ronald Reagan's remarks at the Brandenburg Gate, June 12, 1987

Toward the end of the Cold War, as tensions eased between the United States and the Soviet Union, President Reagan made an historic appearance in Berlin. Standing in front of the Berlin Wall—built in 1961 to stop the mass exodus of people fleeing Soviet East Berlin for West Berlin and the non-Communist world—the American President addressed thousands of Berliners. In the most memorable line of the speech, delivered with an edge of anger in his voice, Ronald Reagan challenged the Soviet leader to demonstrate his commitment to true reform, and destroy the ugly barrier that had separated families and friends for more than a quarter century: "Mr. Gorbachev, tear down this wall."

President Reagan concluded his address that day with a prediction about the fate of the Berlin Wall: "This wall will fall . . . Yes, across Europe, this wall will fall. For it cannot withstand faith. It cannot withstand truth. The wall cannot withstand freedom."
National Archives, Ronald Reagan Presidential Library and Museum, Simi Valley, California

President Ronald Reagan, Berlin, Germany, June 12, 1987

National Archives, Ronald Reagan Presidential Library and Museum, Simi Valley, California

GLOBAL IMPACT

OF THE CHARTERS OF FREEDOM

From the earliest days of the Republic, this nation's Founders believed that the United States had a special mission in the world. George Washington spoke of it on April 30, 1789, moments after taking the oath of office as first President of the United States. "The preservation of the sacred fire of liberty, and the destiny of the Republican model of Government, are justly considered as deeply, perhaps as finally staked, on the experiment entrusted to the hands of the American people." The success of their experiment, these early Americans hoped, would hasten the spread of liberty around the globe.

In the first century following the Declaration of Independence, movements in France, Belgium, Poland, Norway, Switzerland, as well as in Venezuela, Mexico, and Argentina drew both inspiration and practical lessons from the American Revolution and its landmark documents. During the nineteenth century, the adoption of written constitutions often accompanied changes in governments in Europe and Latin America.

In 1917, there were approximately a dozen democracies in the world. Today, there are more than one hundred, and most of them have written constitutions. While the charters of many of these nations vary greatly from the U.S. Constitution, its endurance and stability has surely lent encouragement and credibility to the cause of freedom-loving people everywhere who have labored to throw off tyrannical regimes and devise for themselves a system of self-determination and government based on the consent of the governed.

"The flames kindled on the Fourth of July, 1776,
have spread over too much of the globe
to be extinguished by the feeble engines of despotism;
on the contrary, they will consume these
engines and all who work them."

Thomas Jefferson to John Adams, 1821

"Anti-Communist Demonstration in Prague," photograph by David Turnley, November 1989

On November 9, 1989, the Berlin Wall came down, signaling the collapse of Communism in East Central Europe and the Soviet Union. A series of revolutions captured the world's attention as the peoples of Poland, Hungary, East Germany, Czechoslovakia, and Romania threw off the Communist regimes that had held their countries in an oppressive iron grip for more than forty years.

Weeks after the destruction of the Berlin Wall, at a workers' rally outside Prague, a brewery worker took to the platform and recited words from an earlier revolution:

" 'We hold these truths to be self-evident...' Americans understood these rights more than 200 years ago," he said. "We are only now learning to believe that we are entitled to the same rights."

©David Turnley/Corbis

Quotation Sources

Page 25

"When the last dutiful…"
George Mason, October 2, 1778
The Papers of George Mason, Volume I: 1749–1778.
Robert A. Rutland, Editor. Chapel Hill: University of
North Carolina Press, 1970, p. 436.

Page 29

"Perhaps our Congress will be…"
Abraham Clark, August 6, 1776
*Letters of Delegates to Congress, 1774–1789, Volume IV,
May 16, 1776–August 15, 1776.* Paul H. Smith, Editor.
Gerard W. Gawalt, Rosemary Fry Plakas, Eugene R.
Sheridan, Assistant Editors. Washington, DC:
Library of Congress, 1979, p. 628.

Page 32

"We hold these truths to be self-evident…"
Declaration of Independence, July 4, 1776

Pages 22 and 38

"We have it in our power…"
Thomas Paine, *Common Sense*, February 14, 1776
The Complete Political Works of Thomas Paine, Volume I.
New York: Peter Eckler, Publisher, 1891, pp. 57–58.

Page 41

"I beheld a middle aged African…"
Pennsylvania Packet, February 7, 1774
*Am I Not a Man and a Brother?—The Antislavery
Crusade of Revolutionary America, 1688–1788.* Roger
Bruns, Editor. Foreword by Benjamin Quarles. New
York and London: Chelsea House Publishers in asso-
ciation with R.R. Bowker Company, 1977, p. xix.

Page 45

"[The Constitution] was not, like the fabled Goddess
of Wisdom…"
James Madison, March 10, 1834
Letters and Other Writings of James Madison, Vol. IV.
Philadelphia: J.B. Lippincott & Co., 1865, pp. 341–342.

Page 49

"The sacred rights of mankind…"
Alexander Hamilton, 1775
The Papers of Alexander Hamilton, Volume I: 1768–1778.
Harold C. Syrett, Editor. Jacob E. Cooke, Associate
Editor. New York and London: Columbia University
Press, 1961, p. 122.

Page 63

"The people made the Constitution and the people
can unmake it…"
John Marshall, 1821
Bernard Schwartz. *A Basic History of the Supreme
Court.* Huntington, New York: Robert E. Krieger
Publishing Company, 1968, p. 88.

Page 64

"Let the land rejoice…"
Letter from Gen. Horatio Gates to President Thomas
Jefferson, July 18, 1803, National Archives and
Records Administration, RG 59, General Records of
the Department of State, Applications and
Recommendations for Office, Jefferson, under
Smith, Col. Wm.

Page 71

"The fiery trial through which we pass…"
President Abraham Lincoln's Message to Congress
on the State of the Union, December 1, 1862, National
Archives and Records Administration, RG 46,
Records of the U.S. Senate.

Page 74

"The more men you make free…"
Frederick Douglass, November 17, 1864
*The Frederick Douglass Papers, Series One: Speeches,
Debates, and Interviews. Volume 4: 1864–80.* John W.
Blassingame and John R. McKivigan, Editors. New
Haven and London: Yale University Press, 1979, p.
48.

Page 78

"The bosom of America is open…"
George Washington, December 2, 1783
The Writings of George Washington, Volume 27. John C.
Fitzpatrick, Editor. Washington, DC: United States
Government Printing Office, 1938, p. 254.

Page 83

"It was we, the people…"
Susan B. Anthony, 1873
An Account of the Proceedings on the Trial of Susan B. Anthony
(published in Rochester, NY 1874), p. 152.

Page 85

"We have talked long enough in this country about
equal rights…"
President Lyndon B. Johnson, November 27, 1963
*Public Papers of the Presidents of the United States: Lyndon B.
Johnson, 1963–64, Volume I.* Washington, DC: United
States Government Printing Office, 1965, p. 9.

Page 87

"The flames kindled on the Fourth of July, 1776…"
Thomas Jefferson to John Adams, 1821
The Writings of Thomas Jefferson—Memorial Edition, Vol. XV.
Andrew A. Lipscomb, Editor-in-Chief. Albert Ellery
Bergh, Managing Editor. Washington, DC: The Thomas
Jefferson Memorial Association of the United States, 1904,
p. 334.

Further Reading

Am I Not a Man and a Brother?—The Antislavery Crusade of Revolutionary America, 1688–1788. Roger Bruns, Editor, with a foreword by Benjamin Quarles. New York and London: Chelsea House Publishers, 1977.

Bailyn, Bernard. *Faces of Revolution. Personalities and Themes in the Struggle for American Independence.* New York: Vintage Books, 1990.

Barbash, Fred. *The Founding—A Dramatic Account of the Writing of the Constitution.* New York: Linden Press, 1987.

Becker, Carl. *The Declaration of Independence—A Study in the History of Political Ideas.* New York: Harcourt Brace & Company, 1922.

Bowen, Catherine Drinker. *Miracle at Philadelphia—The Story of the Constitutional Convention, May to September 1787.* Boston: Little, Brown and Company, 1996.

Catton, Bruce. *Reflections on the Civil War.* John Leekley, Editor. Garden City, New York: Doubleday & Company, Inc., 1981.

DeConde, Alexander. *This Affair of Louisiana.* New York: Charles Scribner's Sons, 1976.

Donald, David Herbert. *Lincoln.* New York: Simon & Schuster, 1995.

The Federalist. Jacob E. Cooke, Editor. Hanover, New Hampshire: Wesleyan University Press, 1982.

Franklin, John Hope and Alfred A. Moss, Jr. *From Slavery to Freedom—A History of African Americans.* Eighth Edition. New York: Alfred A. Knopf, 2000.

Hofstadter, Richard. *America at 1750—A Social Portrait.* New York: Vintage Books, 1973.

An Immigrant Nation: United States Regulation of Immigration, 1798–1991. Washington, DC: United States Government Printing Office, 1991.

Jones, Maldwyn Allen. *American Immigration.* Chicago: University of Chicago Press, 1992.

Ketcham, Ralph. *The Anti-Federalist Papers and the Constitutional Convention Debates.* Harmonsworth, Middlesex, England: Penguin Books Ltd., 1986.

Limerick, Patricia Nelson. *The Legacy of Conquest: The Unbroken Past of the American West.* New York: Norton, 1987.

Linder, Doug. *The Trial of Susan B. Anthony for Illegal Voting,* 2001. www.law.umkc.edu/faculty/projects/ftrials/anthony/sbaaccount.html

McCullough, David. *John Adams.* New York: Simon & Schuster, 2001.

McPherson, James. *Battle Cry of Freedom—The Civil War Era.* New York: Oxford University Press, 1988.

Maier, Pauline. *American Scripture—Making the Declaration of Independence.* New York: Alfred A. Knopf, 1997.

Montross, Lynn. *The Reluctant Rebels—The Story of the Continental Congress 1774–1789.* New York: Barnes & Noble, Inc., 1950.

Oates, Stephen B. *With Malice Toward None—The Life of Abraham Lincoln.* New York: Harper & Row, Publishers, 1977.

Schwartz, Bernard. *A Basic History of the Supreme Court.* Huntington, New York: Robert E. Krieger Publishing Company, 1968.

Schwartz, Bernard. *The Great Rights of Mankind—A History of the American Bill of Rights.* Madison, Wisconsin: Madison House Publishers, Inc., 1992.

Wilkins, Roger. *Jefferson's Pillow—The Founding Fathers and the Dilemma of Black Patriotism.* Boston: Beacon Press, 2001.

Wills, Garry. *Inventing America—Jefferson's Declaration of Independence.* Garden City, New York: Doubleday & Company, Inc., 1978.

Wood, Gordon S. *The American Revolution—A History.* A Modern Library Chronicles Book. New York: The Modern Library, 2002.

Acknowledgments

Truth be told, the creation of "A New World Is at Hand"— both the exhibition and this book—was accomplished by scores of people from both inside and outside the National Archives. The exhibition is part of a new series of public programs and exhibits known as the National Archives Experience, whose creation was spearheaded by John W. Carlin, Eighth Archivist of the United States. The planning of this exhibition began with the work of a committee formed in 2000 under the leadership of Marvin Pinkert, Director of Museum Programs. Christina Rudy Smith, Lee Ann Potter, Bruce Bustard, Michael Jackson, Ray Ruskin, and myself—curators, educators, and designers—made up this team whose work was, in part, to identify the main themes to be addressed in the exhibition that would flank the permanent display of the Charters of Freedom in the National Archives Rotunda. As the Rotunda underwent a major renovation that would make these documents more accessible physically, we set out to develop an exhibit that would make their story accessible, accurate, and lively.

We owe a special debt of gratitude to the following historians—some of the nation's foremost experts in their respective fields—for their guidance in this pursuit: Kenneth Bowling, co-editor, *The Documentary History of the First Federal Congress, 1789–1791*; Eric Foner, DeWitt Clinton Professor of History, Columbia University; John Hope Franklin, James B. Duke Professor Emeritus of History, Duke University; James Hutson, Chief, Manuscript Division, Library of Congress; Alfred A. Moss, Jr., Associate Professor of History, University of Maryland; Bruce Ragsdale, Chief Historian, Federal Judicial Center; Roger Wilkins, Clarence J. Robinson Professor of History and American Culture, George Mason University; and Gordon Wood, Alva O. Way University Professor and Professor of History, Brown University. With their vast knowledge, they reviewed the exhibition, either in whole or in part, at various stages in its development, to help ensure the historical accuracy of the story we present to our visitors. These great scholars were uniformly gracious, generous, and deft in their remarks; their contributions cannot be overstated.

The Foundation for the National Archives made this book possible. Thora Colot, Executive Director of the Foundation, initiated this publication and, with the assistance of Stephanie Moore, Thomas Hart, Darlene McClurkin, and intern Elizabeth Bland of the Museum Programs staff, coordinated the entire publication process. Preeminent photographer Carol M. Highsmith created the beautiful pictures of the newly refurbished Rotunda that appear in this book.

The staff of the National Archives and Records Administration is made up of archivists, technicians, conservators, photographers, designers, editors, educators, librarians, as well as specialists in other areas, many of whom made a significant contribution to this project. For many months in 2002–2003, "A New World Is at Hand" was the full-time endeavor of several members of the Museum Programs Staff. Michael Jackson, senior exhibit designer, designed the exhibition; during the summer of 2003, he was assisted by intern Megan Ball. James Zeender was the exhibit registrar who, with the assistance of registrar Karen Hibbitt, safeguarded the documents throughout the exhibit's preparation and installation. Darlene McClurkin conducted picture research, identifying images that complemented the stories revealed in the documents; she also assisted throughout the research and production phases in countless other ways. Senior Conservator Catherine Nicholson led the conservation work, with the assistance of conservator Susan Peckham; Barbara Jo Pilgrim was always helpful and available onsite with conservation assistance during installation and routine maintenance of the exhibit.

Retired senior archivist Milton O. Gustafson may well be the world's expert on the physical history of the Charters and was unfailingly patient and helpful throughout the research, writing, and review of the exhibit manuscript.

From Preservation Programs, Earl McDonald photographed the Charters of Freedom, and Amy Young photographed the other documents displayed; Jeff Reed, Steven Puglia, and Erin Rhodes from the Special Media Preservation Lab scanned the images in preparation for their display and publication.

In the Textual Archives Services Division, archivist Jane Fitzgerald provided physical access to many of the documents over a long period of time; under the direction of Michael Gillette, former director of the National Archives Center for Legislative Archives, and Richard Hunt, Director of the Center, Jessica Kratz provided assistance in gaining access to the legislative documents researched and displayed; Aloha South and Robert Ellis offered valuable guidance through the Records of the Supreme Court; and Michael P. Musick offered guidance on records from the Civil War period. We also thank Mary Ilario of the Special Media Archives Services Division and Jeffrey Hartley of the Archives Library Information Center. Maureen MacDonald copyedited the manuscript for the exhibition and the book; Will Sandoval of the Museum Programs Staff helped name the exhibit, and Catherine Farmer navigated all the administrative matters in connection with it.

The directors and archivists of the regional archives and Presidential libraries, including the staffs of the museums within the libraries, were extremely helpful with suggestions for exhibit items, as well as all kinds of logistical and technical support. We especially thank Shelly Jacobs, John Langellier, and Leslie Rankin at the Ronald Reagan Library; Mary Warren and Amy Day at the George Bush Library; and Alycia Vivona at the Franklin D. Roosevelt Library. The late Robert Morris, former director of the Northeast regional archives in New York City was always helpful in providing guidance on the records relating to Susan B. Anthony, as was John Celardo, also from New York. Douglas Thurman of the Office of Presidential Libraries and Nancy Malan of the Office of Regional Records Services facilitated our work with the libraries and regions. Many senior level man-agers at the National Archives participated in the exhibit review process, offering insightful comments and suggestions: Lori Lisowski, Director, Policy and Communications Staff; John Constance, Director, Congressional and Public Affairs Staff; Susan Cooper, Director of Public Affairs; Michael Kurtz, Assistant Archivist for the Office of Records Services, Washington, DC; Adrienne Thomas, Assistant Archivist for the Office of Administrative Services; and Richard Claypoole, Assistant Archivist for the Office of Presidential Libraries.

Outside the National Archives, I would like to thank Paul Davis of West Chester, Pennsylvania, who shared his knowledge of illustrator Howard Pyle, and Greg Marcangelo of the Prints and Photographs Division of the Library of Congress. Finally, I thank Phil McCombs, a true patriot, for sharing his exuberance, ideas, and wisdom.

It is not possible to name all the hundreds of people whose work and talents brought "A New World Is at Hand" to completion, but I thank them all wholeheartedly.

Stacey Bredhoff, Curator

Index

THE BIG BRAIN
WORKOUT

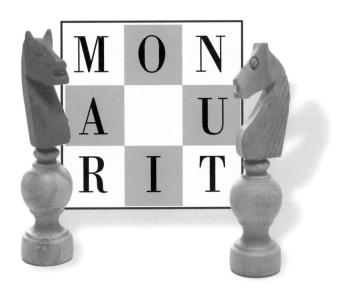

Copy or trace the black lines onto stiff board and cut out the pieces.
You'll add hours more pleasure, puzzling out the 20 Tangrams
that serve here as intriguing openers to our puzzle sections.
From the book TANGRAM by Jerry Slocum, published by Sterling.
This portrait of King Henry IV of France (1575–1610) was published
as a Tangram puzzle in 1818 in Paris.

JACK BOTERMANS / HELEEN TICHLER

THE BIG BRAIN
WORKOUT

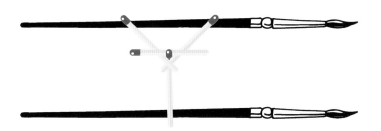

Sterling Publishing Co., Inc.
New York

What does this mean?

Compilation and text by Jack Botermans and Heleen Tichler
Illustrations and design by Jack Botermans
Puzzle cards from the collection of Jerry Slocum, Beverly Hills, USA.
Translated from the Dutch by Carla van Splunteren
English edition edited by Claire Bazinet

Library of Congress Cataloging-in-Publication Data Available

10 9 8 7 6 5 4 3

Published by Sterling Publishing Co., Inc.
387 Park Avenue South, New York, NY 10016
© 2005 by Sterling Publishing Co., Inc.
© 2003 by Bookman International, by Laren and Jack Botermans,
Amsterdam, The Netherlands
Tangram figures © 2003 from the book *Tangram* by Jerry Slocum

Distributed in Canada by Sterling Publishing c/o Canadian Manda Group
165 Dufferin Street, Toronto, Ontario, Canada M6K 3H6
Distributed in the United Kingdom by GMC Distribution Sservices,
Castle Place, 166 High Street, Lewes, East Sussex, England BN7 1XU
Distributed in Australia by Capricorn Link (Australia) Pty. Ltd.
P.O. Box 704, Windsor, NSW 2756, Australia

For information about custom editions, special sales, premium and
corporate purchases, please contact Sterling Special Sales
Department at 800-805-5489 or specialsales@sterlingpub.com.

Printed in China
All rights reserved

Sterling ISBN-13: 978-1-4027-2210-3
        ISBN-10: 1-4027-2210-9

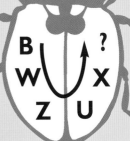

Contents

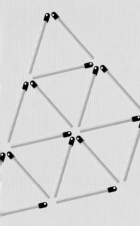

5

THE BIG BRAIN WORKOUT

Complete with Puzzles Competition

Puzzles keep the mind active and agile. Albert Einstein, for example, always had a few puzzles close at hand, and made it a point to keep in frequent contact with the puzzle experts of his time. Research has since proven that it is even possible to improve certain brain functions by regularly solving puzzles that stimulate your gray matter. So, this book is the result of our overriding purpose: To keep Alzheimer's at bay! Improving mental agility by solving puzzles is also a wonderful alternative to simply vegetating in front of a TV screen.

This book, containing over two hundred puzzles, also provides an excellent opportunity to organize a fun-filled and exhilarating competition—as you "flex your brain muscles" together. We've provided, on every sixth page, a score sheet to note down the results. Although the puzzles vary from easy to difficult, those are relative concepts; as individuals tend to excel or do less well in various areas. How well do you measure up? How do you compare overall to family and friends? Find out by solving the puzzles in this book—and having fun doing it!

The Scoring

Everyone should try to solve the puzzles in each section at his or her own pace, making note of their answers on a sheet of paper. Once everyone is finished, write down the name of each participant on the score sheet at the end of the puzzle section. Compare the results against the solutions given next to the score sheet.

If your answer is right, put a mark next to your name in the column of the puzzle you got correct. Each participant's points are then added up and entered at the far right. Later, these results will be recorded on the final score sheet at the back of the book.

Take as much time as you want to complete each puzzle in the section. It's not even necessary for everyone to solve the puzzles at the same time. New participants can simply start at the beginning, and friends or far-flung family members who have a copy of the book can each use their own, then enter and compare scores with those of other puzzlers.

For extra puzzling pleasure, each puzzle section begins with a Tangram puzzle. It can be solved with the help of the Tangram pieces you see across from the title page. Trace or copy the pieces, cut out your copies, and use them to try to solve the Tangrams. The illustrations are from the book *Tangram* by Jerry Slocum, also published by Sterling. Should these Tangram puzzles arouse your interest, you can discover over 1600 others in *Tangram*.

SECTION I

THE BIG BRAIN WORKOUT

1 THE MAVERICK

B X G R K

Which of these letters does not belong?

2 MAXIMUM WEIGHT

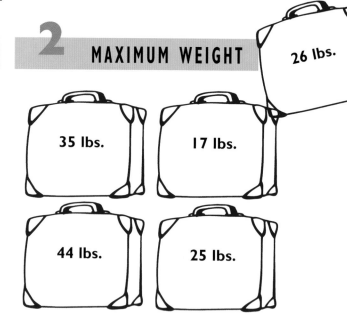

26 lbs.

35 lbs.

17 lbs.

44 lbs.

25 lbs.

Of these five suitcases, one does not belong. Which one is it?

3 FITTING AND MEASURING

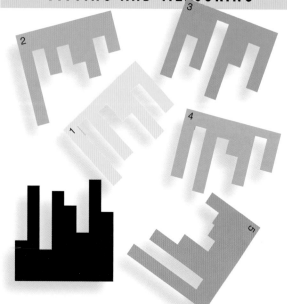

Which form fits into the black one?

4 NASTY INKBLOTS

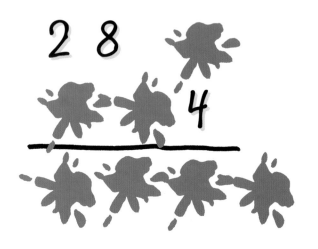

2 8

4

Ooops! Inkblots have blocked out some numbers. In this problem, every number between 1 through 9 was used once. Can you reconstruct the addition?

5 CLEVER

$$24-9-25-2-15-17$$
$$2-6-11-16-17-2-6-11$$

He was a very clever man, and even received a Nobel Prize. But he was the first to understand that everything is relative. Can you figure out who we're talking about?

7 MATCHBOX PUZZLE

Puzzle by Oskar van Deventer
Illustration by Wico Vos

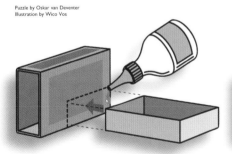

This is a puzzle that can be done in turns. First, to make the puzzle, you need five empty matchboxes. Open them and glue the five together as shown. Now try to assemble each puzzle piece so that each "box" part fits into a lid.

End result by David van Dijk

6 COIN SWEEPING

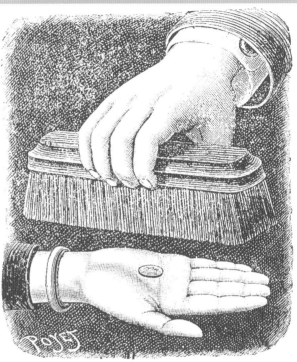

Is it possible to sweep a small coin from the palm of your hand with a brush?

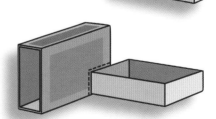

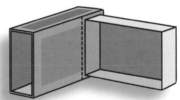

8 COIN PUZZLE

Make a square of 16 coins, four rows of four, heads and tails in turn. Now try to change the heads and tails in all four rows by only touching two coins.

9 WHO IS THE TALLEST?

Two people are waiting for the train. Who is the tallest? Try to figure it out before measuring them!

10 TWENTY-SEVEN LEGS

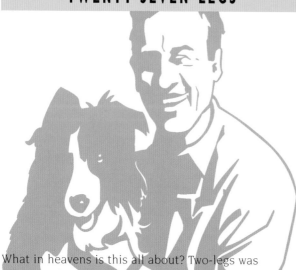

What in heavens is this all about? Two-legs was sitting on three-legs when four-legs came by and stole a leg. Two-legs took the three-legs and threw it at four-legs. Then four-legs dropped one leg. Two-legs went over, picked up one-leg and ate it.

11 FIND THE CANDIDATE

In the United States, a series of picture puzzles was published in 1880 that had the faces of the then presidential candidates hidden in them. This picture has such a face, can you find the candidate?

12 ROBIN HOODS

Two of these Robin Hoods are identical twins. Can you find out which ones they are?

1 THE MAVERICK
The X does not belong. It's the only letter with a serif.

2 MAXIMUM WEIGHT
The suitcase weighing 25 lbs. The numbers of the other suitcases all total eight (example 3+5, 1+7, etc.).

3 FITTING AND MEASURING
Number 4

4 NASTY INKBLOTS

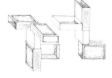

5 CLEVER
Albert Einstein. The numbers indicate the position of the letters in the alphabet, but then three was deducted from each number. From A you go back to Z.

6 COIN SWEEPING
You will discover that it is impossible to brush a coin out of your hand.

7 MATCHBOX PUZZLE

8 COIN PUZZLE
Push two coins from the top row to the bottom, then push those rows upward.

9 WHO IS THE TALLEST?
Both men are the same height.

10 TWENTY-SEVEN LEGS
A man is sitting on a tripod holding a leg of lamb. A dog comes by and steals the leg. The man throws the tripod at the dog. The dog drops the leg. The man picks up the leg and continues eating his piece of meat. Simple, no?

11 FIND THE CANDIDATE
Turn the picture to the right!

12 ROBIN HOODS
Number 2 from the first row and number 4 from the second row.

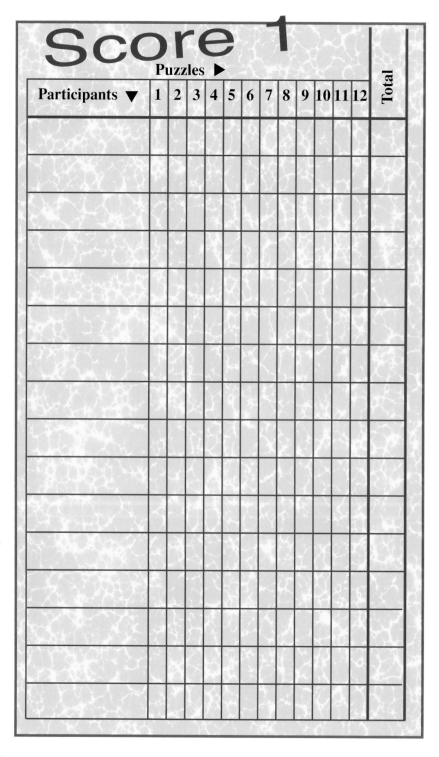

Participants ▼	1	2	3	4	5	6	7	8	9	10	11	12	Total

SECTION 2

THE BIG BRAIN WORKOUT

1 TRAVELING

Hank is on a trip through the Netherlands. He thought Amsterdam was a nice city, but Groningen was less interesting than he'd anticipated. Leeuwarden, on the other hand, was OK. Heerlen was a bummer. After a nice visit to Amersfoort he got kind of bored in Nederveen. Did he think Alkmaar was a nice city?

2 LETTER PROBLEMS

What letter belongs in the box with the question mark?

3 WORK OF ART

24-3-16
9-17-9-10

Can you figure out who painted this work of art?

4 CUBE PUZZLE

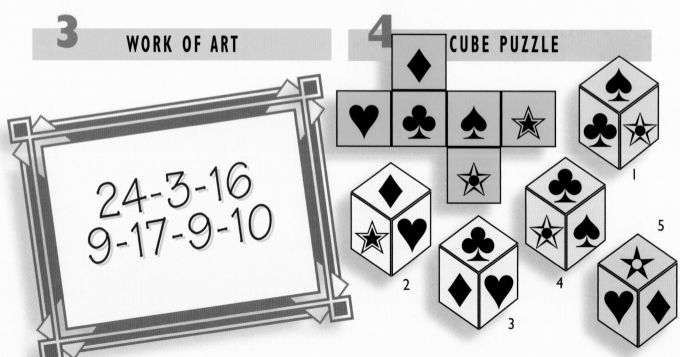

Which of these cubes cannot be made with the folding plan pictured here?

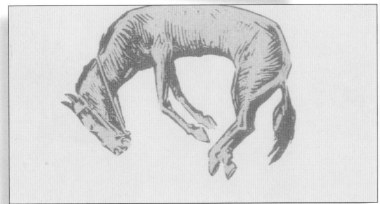

5 RODEO

Copy the page and cut out the three illustrations. Then try to position the brave cowboys on their horses without folding or ripping.

6 PICTURE PUZZLE

In this landscape find the antelope, the wolf, the bat and the flamingo.

7 BALLS

Which ball does not belong with the others?

8 COIN PUZZLE

With 21 coins, make twelve rows of five coins.

9 MATCHES

Can you correct this sequence? You only need to change the position of two matches.

10 MIKADO

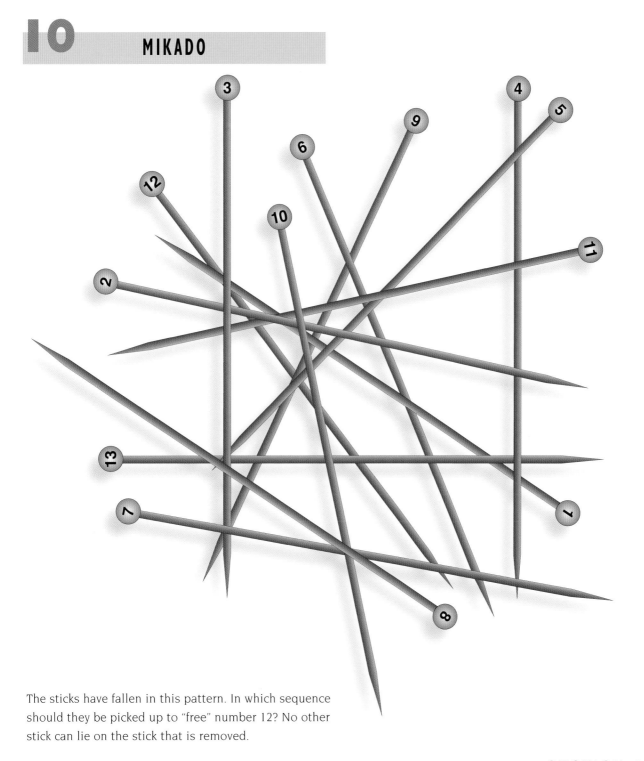

The sticks have fallen in this pattern. In which sequence should they be picked up to "free" number 12? No other stick can lie on the stick that is removed.

THE BIG BRAIN WORKOUT

1 TRAVELING
Hank liked all the cities with the letter A in the name. He did not like the other cities. So Hank thought Alkmaar was nice.

2 LETTER PROBLEMS
B. The letters are in alphabetical order, but a letter is skipped between them. The sequence runs from top left to the bottom, then second column upward, etc.

3 WORK OF ART
Van Gogh. The numbers correspond to their positions in the alphabet plus 2. So 24=X. X-2=22=V, etc.

4 CUBE PUZZLE
Number five!

5 RODEO

6 PICTURE PUZZLE

7 BALLS
15, for that is the only number that can be divided by 3 and 5. The other numbers are not divisible.

8 COIN PUZZLE

9 MATCHES

V+V=X

10 MIKADO
8-10-7-3-2-11-5-4-13-1-6-9-12

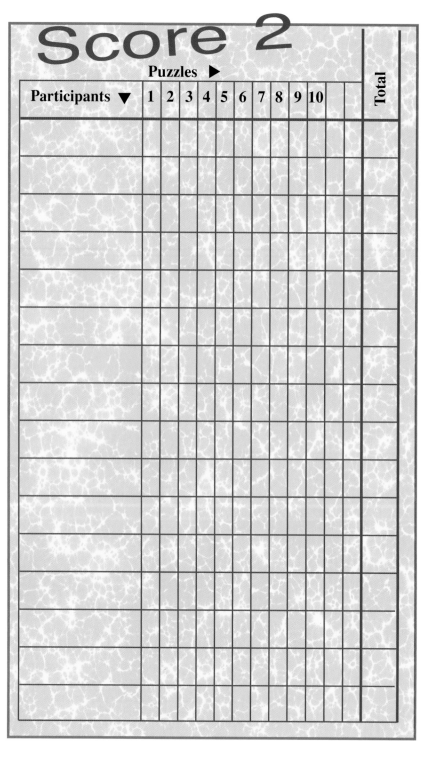

Score 2														Total
Participants ▼	1	2	3	4	5	6	7	8	9	10				

Puzzles ▶

PUZZLE SECTION 3

The Big Brain Workout

1 POSITIONING

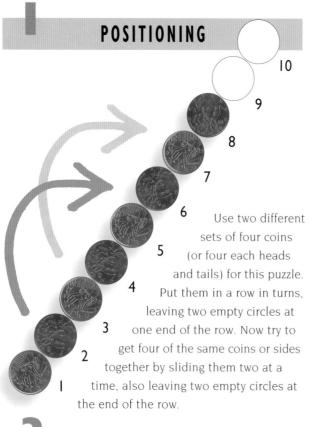

Use two different sets of four coins (or four each heads and tails) for this puzzle. Put them in a row in turns, leaving two empty circles at one end of the row. Now try to get four of the same coins or sides together by sliding them two at a time, also leaving two empty circles at the end of the row.

2 JUGGLING WITH CARAFES

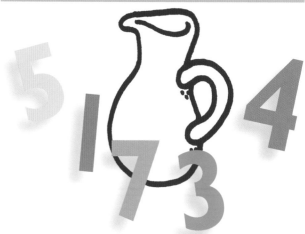

You have three water jugs, and you know that they can contain three, four and seven liters of water. This, however, is not indicated on the carafes themselves. The big carafe is full, and you want to pour five liters out of it. How do you manage to get the five liters in total in one carafe while pouring from one into the other as few times as possible?

3 DOUBLE LETTERS

An old-fashioned typewriter was used and, as you can see, there are some problems. The words have been typed on top of each other. Can you figure out what the words are?

4 FAMILY

Recently, an old lady ran into a man. The man said to her "I think I know you." The lady said that was highly probable, because his mother was the only daughter of her mother. How are these two people related?

5 STRANGE?

Two individuals are born in the same place at the same time. After 50 years they both die, also in the same place. Nevertheless, one of the two lived a hundred days longer than the other one. How did this remarkable situation come about?

6 PYRAMIDS

Move two matches and leave four triangles and a rhomboid.

7 CHEERS

OÙ SONT LES BUVEURS ?

Where are the two drinkers? A *devinette* (picture puzzle) from France, circa 1890.

8 PRESIDENTS

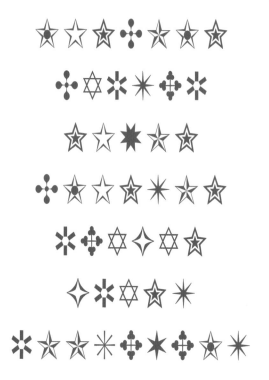

The names of seven American presidents are listed above. What are they? Each star represents a letter.

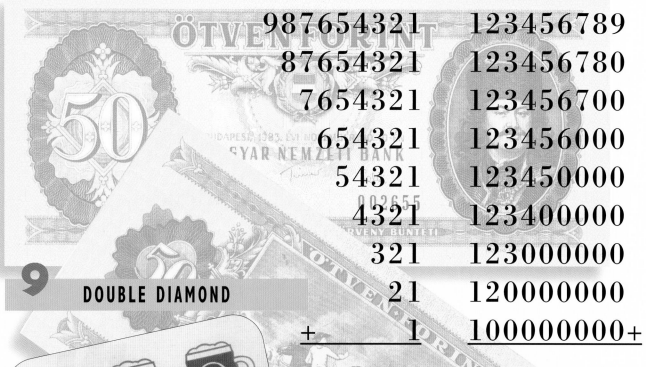

```
987654321        123456789
 87654321        123456780
  7654321        123456700
   654321        123456000
    54321        123450000
     4321        123400000
      321        123000000
       21        120000000
+       1        100000000+
```

9 DOUBLE DIAMOND

Guess which trail leads to the DD? If you get it right, treat yourself to a pint.

Which trail leads to the Double Diamond pint? A Double Diamond advertising coaster from the 1990s, Great Britain.

10 FORINTS

While paying a visit to Hungary, you need many forints; although the euro will soon change all that. So here is a puzzle with forints and euros. Assuming the numbers in the right column represent Hungarian forints, and the numbers in the left one represent euros, which sum do you prefer, the one on the left or the one on the right?

THE BIG BRAIN WORKOUT

1 POSITIONING
Move 2 and 3 to 9 and 10. 5 and 6 to 2 and 3.
8 and 9 to 5 and 6. 1 and 2 to 8 and 9.

2 JUGGLING WITH CARAFES
You will have to pour seven times.

	3 l. jug	4 l. jug	7 l. jug
-	0	0	7
1	0	4	3
2	3	1	3
3	0	1	6
4	1	0	6
5	1	4	2
6	3	2	2
7	0	2	5

3 DOUBLE LETTERS
Crusoe - Friday
Cain - Abel
Phoenix - Wichita
Arkansas - Nebraska

4 FAMILY
He is her son.

5 STRANGE?
Both people used to travel around the
world once a year, but one traveled
westward and the other eastward. The
person traveling west gained one day on
each trip, while the person traveling east
lost a day each trip, due to the different
time zones. In 50 years, that amounts
to 100 days.

6 PYRAMIDS

7 CHEERS

8 PRESIDENTS
Lincoln, Carter, Nixon, Clinton,
Reagan, Grant, Roosevelt.

9 DOUBLE DIAMOND
The trail on the left.

10 FORINTS
Each column adds up to the same amount:
1,083,676,269. However, in terms of value
the euros do a bit better.

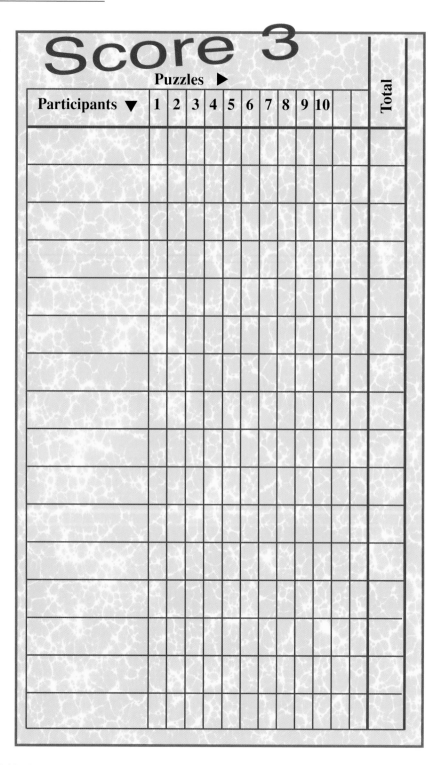

Participants ▼	1	2	3	4	5	6	7	8	9	10		Total

Score 3

Puzzles ▶

SECTION 4

THE BIG BRAIN WORKOUT

1 PREHISTORY

15 6 2 15 5 6 19 21 9 2 13

He walked around Europe in prehistoric times. These days, however, his name is more of a derogatory term for someone who isn't very bright. Are you like him, or are you more developed?

2 POOL

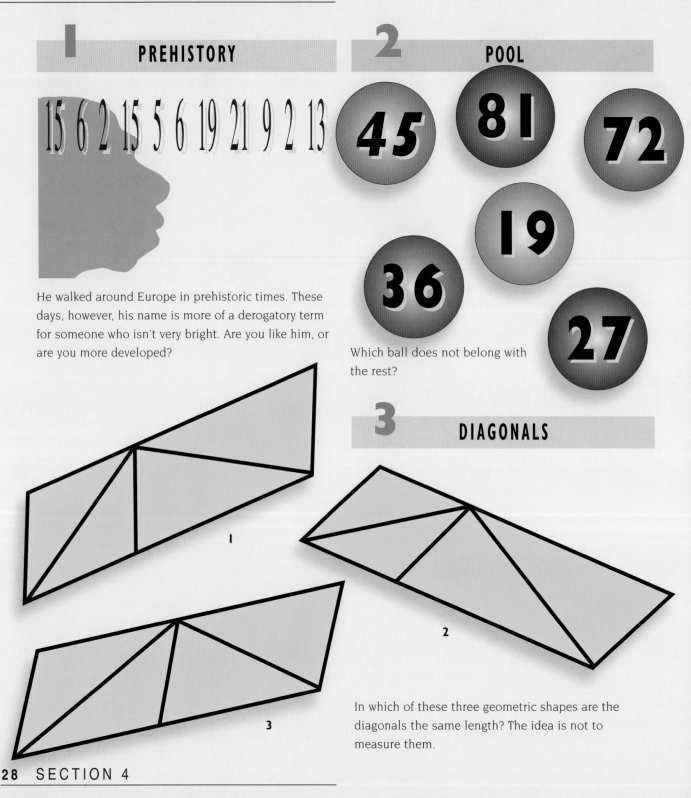

Which ball does not belong with the rest?

3 DIAGONALS

In which of these three geometric shapes are the diagonals the same length? The idea is not to measure them.

4 TRIP THROUGH FRANCE

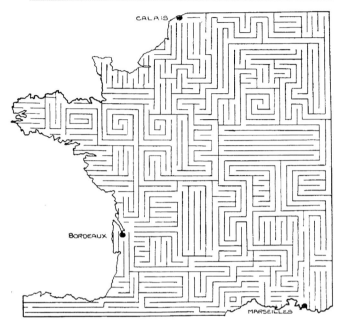

Take a trip from Marseilles to Calais, and then on to Bordeaux and back to Marseilles. Cover the labyrinth with a piece of tracing paper, and check your solution.

5 THE SNAIL, THE PEARS AND THE CHILD

Find the child.

6 FIVE IN A ROW

Take eight coins and position them as indicated. Can you arrange five coins in a row in every direction while replacing just one coin?

7 SQUARE OF NUMBERS

If you write the figures 1 through 12 in the empty squares in exactly the right positions, the sum of all the vertical rows will be 26. And if you can do it in such a way that the sum of the six outside squares is also 26, you're really clever!

8 RECTANGLES

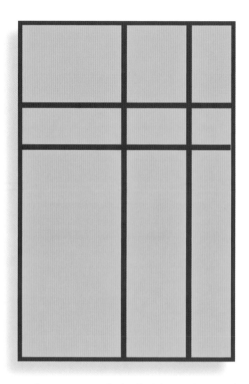

You know what a rectangle looks like, right? Looking at the illustration above, how many rectangles do you see?

9 "FUN" CAR RIDE

At exactly 7 o'clock on the morning of Saturday March 8, 1934, Hal Warner, a very punctual man, drove to church. It took him 13 minutes. Exactly 60 minutes later he drove to his friend's house at 45 miles per hour. Unfortunately, six miles away from his friend's house he broke down due to an empty gas tank. What time was it?

10 ROTHSCHILD

The garden of the Rothschild castle has marvelous old trees. Four old beeches surround the beautiful swimming pool in the garden. The baron wishes to double the size of his swimming pool without having to chop down the beeches. How should he do that?

THE BIG BRAIN WORKOUT

1 PREHISTORY

Neanderthal. The numbers correspond with
the position of the letters in the alphabet,
but have been moved up one place.

2 POOL

19, for the figures of all the other numbers
add up to 9.

3 DIAGONALS

Illustration 1 has diagonals of the same
length.

4 TRIP THROUGH FRANCE

5 THE SNAIL, THE PEARS
AND THE CHILD

6 FIVE IN A ROW

Place the fifth coin from the right on top of
the coin in the corner.

7 SQUARE OF
NUMBERS

8 RECTANGLES

If you add up all the rectangles you have
26 rectangles.

9 "FUN" CAR RIDE

One thing is for sure: it was time to go
look for gas.

10 ROTHSCHILD

Participants ▼	1	2	3	4	5	6	7	8	9	10	Total

Score 4
Puzzles ▶

1 GENDARMES ON THE LOOKOUT

These gentlemen are looking for two villains. Can you help find them?

2 NOT JUST A TRIANGLE!

A •   • C

• B

Draw a triangle. That shouldn't be a problem. But points A, B and C should each be in the middle of one side. Remember how that works? Use a piece of tracing paper to find the solution.

3 GEOGRAPHY

Abebbew

Madrich

Africe

Mexica

That old typewriter has been at it again! Here, the words are all geographic names that have the same "neighbors" or are "neighbors."

4 A LARGE FAMILY

In a family with nine daughters, all the daughters have a brother. This family consists of how many members?

5 THE ROYAL TRIO

Optimal concentration is needed here!

A. To the right of the king there are one or two queens.

B. To the left of one queen there are one or two queens.

C. To the left of the hearts there are one or two spades.

D. To the right of one spade there are one or two spades.

What are these three cards?

6 FITTING AND MEASURING

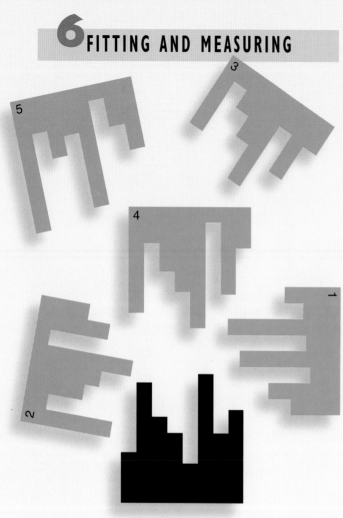

Which figure fits onto the black one?

8 MOON IS MADE OF GREEN CHEESE?

Attention! There's a farm in a provence in the south of France that has the best pear orchard in the world. The average tree there has exactly 24 branches, each branch has exactly 12 side branches, each side branch exactly 6 shoots and each shoot bears exactly one fruit. How many apples grow on each tree?

7 9 WHICH NUMBER?

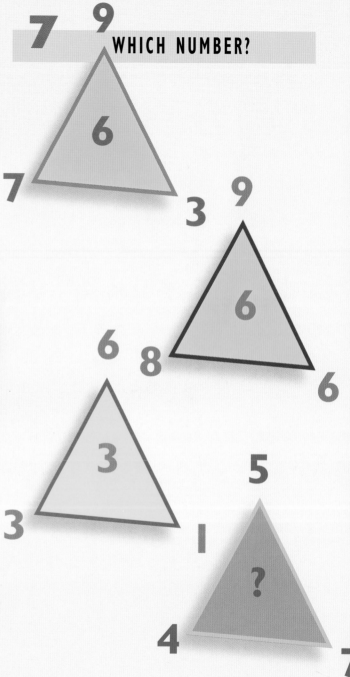

Which number should be in the center of the bottom triangle?

9 NUMBER 13

12	3	6	4	5	4	9	7	10	X
9	9	10	8	1	12	5	3	7	4
3	5	12	10	10	6	3	1	8	10
9	4	4	9	8	5	9	9	11	9
10	3	5	5	3	11	8	7	10	3
6	12	8	7	10	2	6	6	1	7
4	9	5	4	4	9	4	8	2	4
7	11	8	2	3	7	11	7	2	6
5	1	4	X	8	2	X	9	6	8
1	4	8	6	8	9	7	5	9	X

Using tracing paper, each time you find two numbers on the same horizontal or vertical line that add up to 13, cross them out. See the examples above. At the end, four numbers remain. Which ones?

THE BIG BRAIN WORKOUT

1 GENDARMES ON THE LOOKOUT

2 NOT JUST A TRIANGLE!

Draw a line through A, parallel to BC. Then draw a line through B parallel to AC. The last line is through C parallel to AB.

3 GEOGRAPHY

Aberdeen – Heathrow
Madrid – London
Europe – Africa
Canada – Mexico

4 A LARGE FAMILY

If father and mother are still alive, it is a family of 12.

5 THE ROYAL TRIO

A tells us card number 3 cannot be a king.
B tells us card number 2 cannot be a king.
That is why card 1 must be a king.
C tells us cards number 1 and 2 cannot both be hearts.
D tells us two spades are lying side by side.
This means cards 1 and 2 are spades.
Thus the only correct answer is:
  Card 1 – spade king
  Card 2 – spade queen
  Card 3 – queen of hearts
So, as you see, the king is right where he should be, next to his wife.

6 FITTING AND MEASURING

No. 2.

7 WHICH NUMBER?

7. The top number minus the bottom left number multiplied by the bottom right number.

8 MOON IS MADE OF GREEN CHEESE?

No apples can grow on a pear tree!

9 NUMBER THIRTEEN

1, 7, 8 and 9.

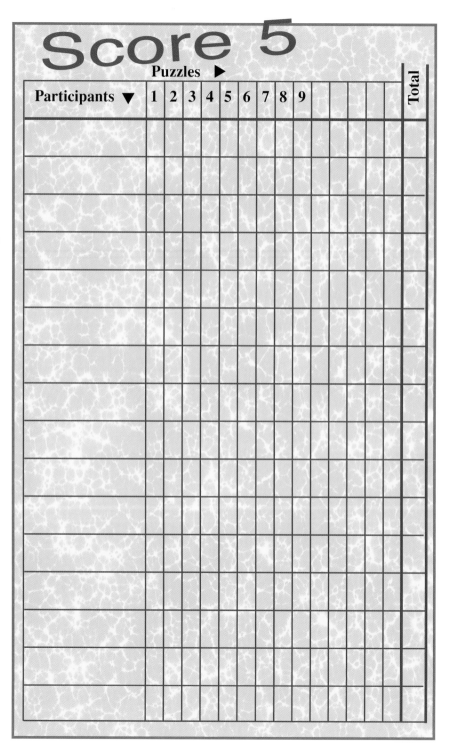

Participants ▼	1	2	3	4	5	6	7	8	9					Total

Score 5
Puzzles ▶

Who is the smartest? Who is the smartest?

THE BIG BRAIN WORKOUT

1 TRIANGLE

Can you make the triangle point upwards by moving only three coins?

2 DICE TOWERS

Two "towers" of four dice. What is the total number of pips on the invisible upper and bottom sides?

3 FRACTURED FRACTION?

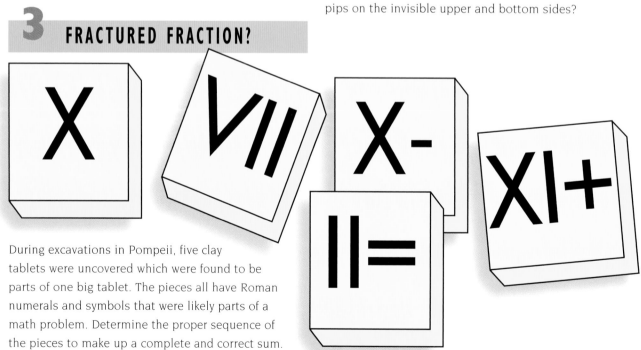

During excavations in Pompeii, five clay tablets were uncovered which were found to be parts of one big tablet. The pieces all have Roman numerals and symbols that were likely parts of a math problem. Determine the proper sequence of the pieces to make up a complete and correct sum.

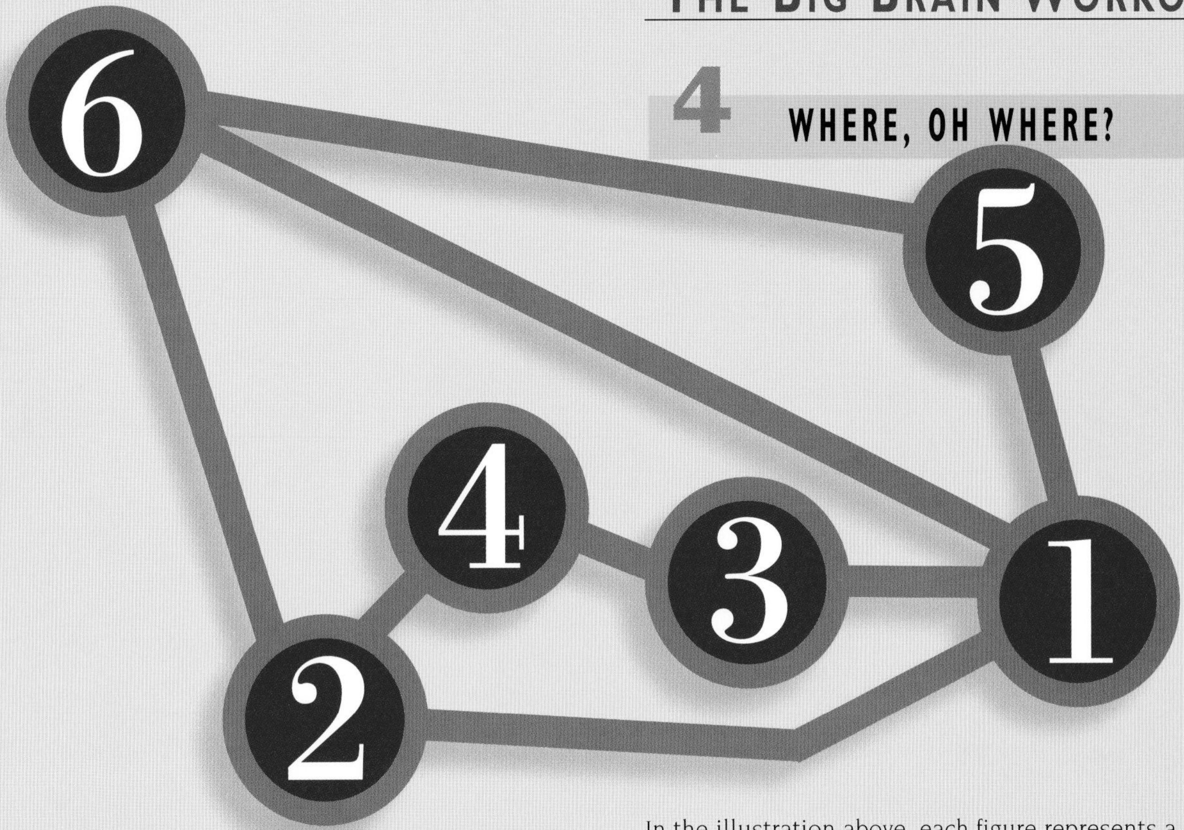

4 WHERE, OH WHERE?

In the illustration above, each figure represents a letter. If A is only connected with B, C and D, and C is only connected with A and E, where should F be?

5 MON-STAR

In Japan, this star is known as a "mon." It is often used for things such as a family coat of arms. At first sight, you might say you need eight square sheets of paper to make this "mon," but maybe that's a bit much? How many square sheets of paper are actually needed here?

6 SEQUENCES

0 1 2 2 2 3 8 9 2 3 2

With the figures given above, make a sequence of successive numbers. You need only use nine of the ten figures.

7 RUNNING CHICKENS?

Pretend you have to pass a test before you could run a chicken farm. You are asked to put 25 chickens into six runs, but with an uneven number of chickens in each run. Would you pass the test? What is the solution?

8 SIMPLE?

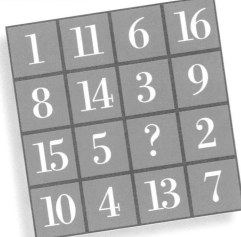

Can you figure out what number belongs in the box with the question mark?

10 MENAGERIE

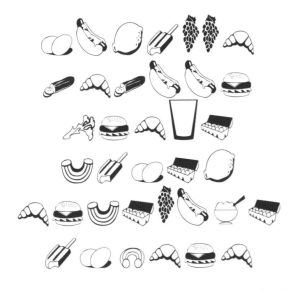

Crack this food code to find the names of animals. The grapes stand for the letter L, the hotdog for O.

9 CHARITY PARTY

In New York, a big party was organized, the proceeds of which were to go to charity. The party was attended by 1200 people, who paid a total of $24,000 in admission fees. The men each paid $100 admission, the women $40 and the children $2. How many men, women and children were at the party?

THE BIG BRAIN WORKOUT

1 TRIANGLE

The bottom coin moves to the top. The two side-corner coins go to the bottom.

2 DICE TOWERS

The sum of two opposite sides of a dice is seven. 8 x 7 is 56. If you deduct what is on the two visible top sides (1+3) the total is 52.

3 FRACTURED FRACTION?

XI+II=XX-VII

4 WHERE, OH WHERE?

F should be on 5. 1 = B or D. 2 = A, 3 = E, 4 = C, 5 = F, 6 = B or D.

5 MON-STAR

Only two, provided with diagonal notches, with one paper sheet having a diagonal cut all the way to the corner.

6 SEQUENCES

Without the 8: 229, 230, 231.

7 RUNNING CHICKENS?

You make five runs and put five chickens in each run, then around your five runs you add a sixth run.

8 SIMPLE?

12. The square is a magic square, which means that all the columns, rows and diagonals have the same sum, in this case 34.

9 CHARITY PARTY

170 men, 130 women and 900 children.

10 MENAGERIE

gorilla, baboon, snake, tiger, antelope, and iguana

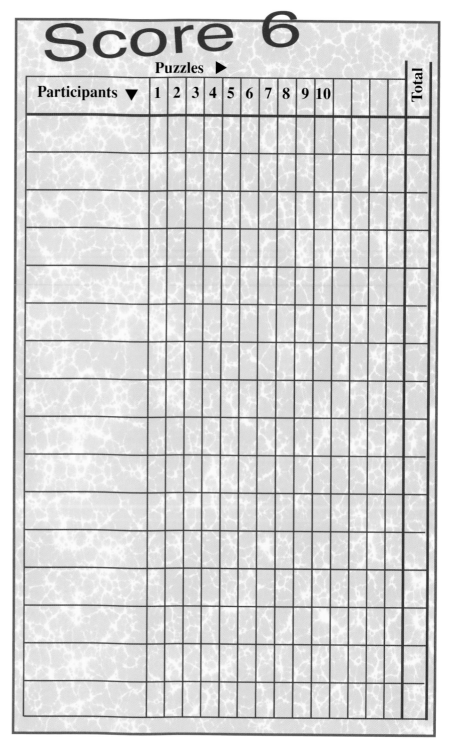

SECTION 7

Who is the smartest? Who is the smartest?

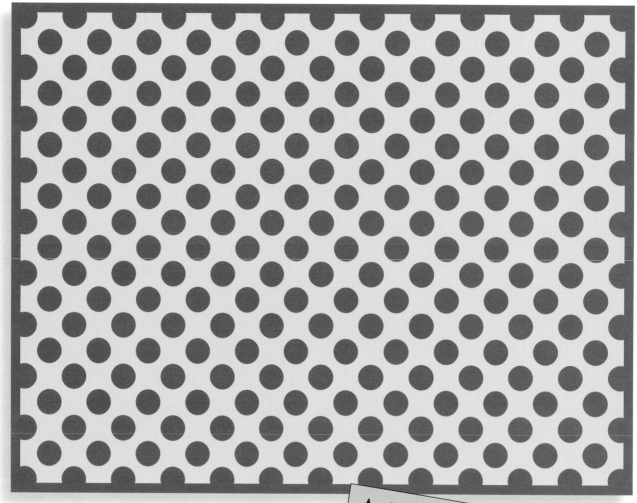

A B C D E F G H
I J K M N O P Q
R S T U V W X Y Z

1   ESTIMATION

You won't go dotty from seeing all these dots, but there are many of them. The question is: how many? Try to estimate—without counting—how many dots you see. If you are like most people, you won't even come close. Not even down to 20 close.

Note: The semi-dots around the edges don't count; they are only there to make life more difficult for you.

2   AMERICAN

This is a greeting card. But what kind of greeting card is it, and what does it say?

3 TIRE TROUBLE

A driver has tire trouble and wants to replace the flat tire with the spare one. But while doing this, he loses four nuts. The driver wants to get new nuts at the nearest service station. How does he drive there?

4 A BILLION

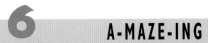

You ask someone to count out one billion dollars for you. If it takes that person one second to count one dollar while working eight hours a day, minus four weeks holiday a year, how long will your money counter be busy counting the billion?

5 THE MATCH PIG

Take a box of matches and lay out the following puzzle. By replacing two of the matches, make the pig look around.

6 A-MAZE-ING

Bring the two lovers together. An American postcard from 1930.

THE BIG BRAIN WORKOUT

7 MYSTERIOUS CITIES

Which European capitals are mentioned here?

8 PRESIDENT

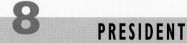

Find the presidential candidate. A publication from 1880, America.

9 A BRIDGE

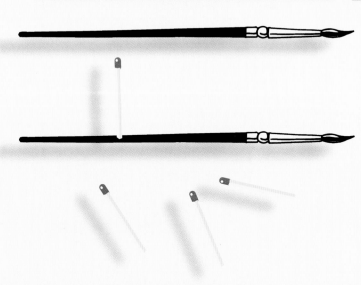

With only these four matches, try to build a solid bridge between these two pencils.

10 VISUAL ILLUSIONS

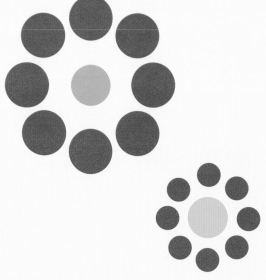

Which of the two inner circles is bigger, and which of the two is the lightest in color?

 ## CAKE!

A truly beautiful cake, don't you think? Although you'd like to keep the whole thing for yourself, you unfortunately have to share it with seven friends. The cake is 4 inches thick and has a diameter of 12 inches. How do you divide it into eight same-size pieces while only cutting it three times?

1 ESTIMATION
The correct number is 196 dots.

2 AMERICAN
It is a British Christmas card and it says:
"Noel"—there's "no L" on the card. ("Noel"'
is another word for Christmas.)

3 TIRE TROUBLE
He undoes one nut from each of the
other three tires and then uses these three
nuts for the spare tire.

4 A BILLION
If the person works five days a week and 48
weeks a year, it will take him 144 years.

5 THE MATCH PIG

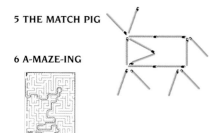

6 A-MAZE-ING

7 MYSTERIOUS CITIES
Dublin
Brussels
Madrid
Paris
Berlin

8 PRESIDENT
Turn the print to the right.

9 A BRIDGE

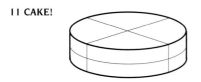

10 VISUAL ILLUSIONS
Both are the same size and the same color.

11 CAKE!

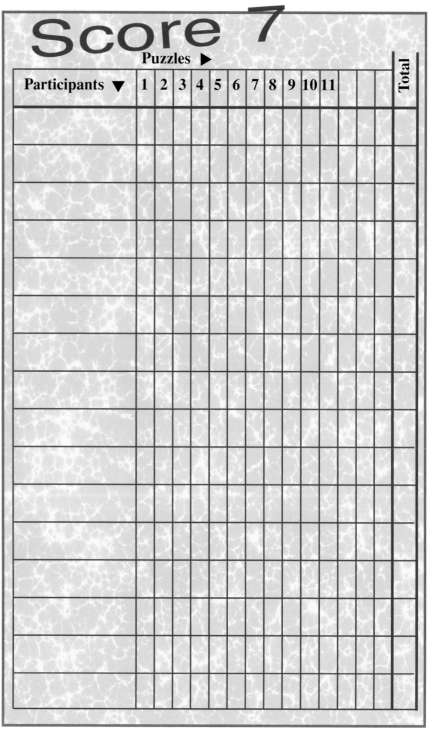

Score 7

Participants ▼	Puzzles ▶														Total
	1	2	3	4	5	6	7	8	9	10	11				

SECTION 8

THE BIG BRAIN WORKOUT

1 TRIANGLES

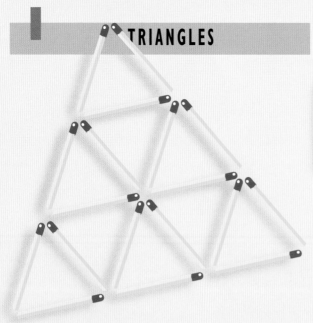

Take away 5 matches in order to get five triangles.

2 AS HIGH AS POSSIBLE

Move the numbers around until they are positioned in such a way that if multiplied they add up to the highest possible sum.

3 FITTING AND MEASURING

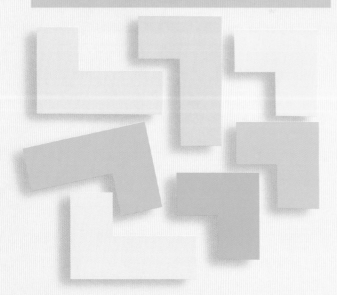

Trace the figures, cut them out and try to make a square out of them.

4 DISTURBING STAINS

You multiply by 2 a number that consists of all the figures from 0 through 9, then you miraculously again have a number in which all the figures from 0 through 9 are used just once. Not only is it possible, there are even several solutions.

5 A BIKE RIDE

Nelly bikes to see her mother every week. Her mother lives nearby. Today she starts out at a brisk clip of 24 kilometers an hour until one tire goes flat when she is about halfway there. Nelly walks two kilometers, which takes her exactly half an hour. Then she gets a lift, which takes her to her mom at the speed of eight kilometers an hour. It takes her one and a half hours in total to reach her mother's house. How far away from her mom does she live?

6 TRICKY!

11 23 11
10 24 13
13 33 ?

What number belongs in place of the question mark?

7 MADE-TO-MEASURE

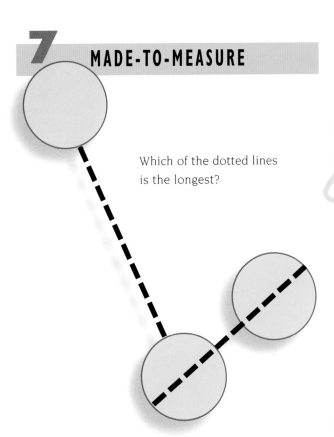

Which of the dotted lines is the longest?

8 CHICKEN LOGIC

In four chicken coops, 25 hens hatch 40 eggs in 18 days. How many days do 20 hens in six chicken coops need to hatch 40 eggs?

9 A ROUND NUMBER

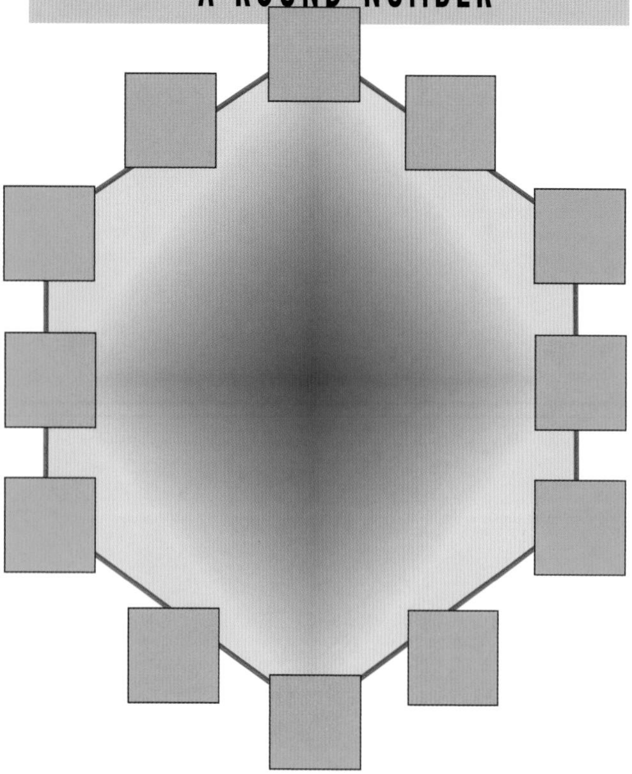

The depicted hexagon has three empty areas per side and 12 areas in all. Fill in these empty areas, with the numbers 1 through 12. Do it in such a way that the sum of the numbers per side (each of the six sides) is the same.

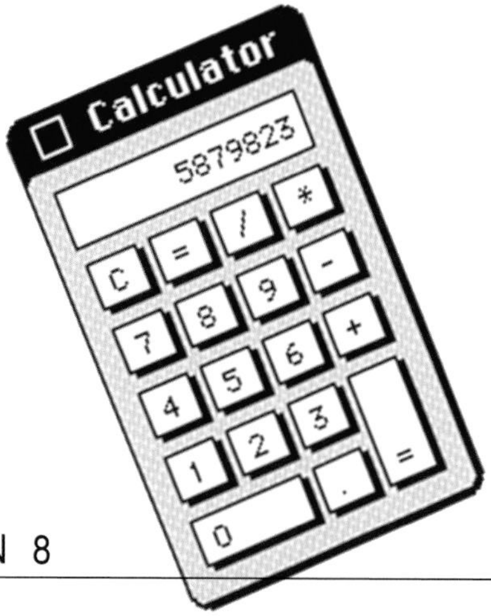

10 FOURS

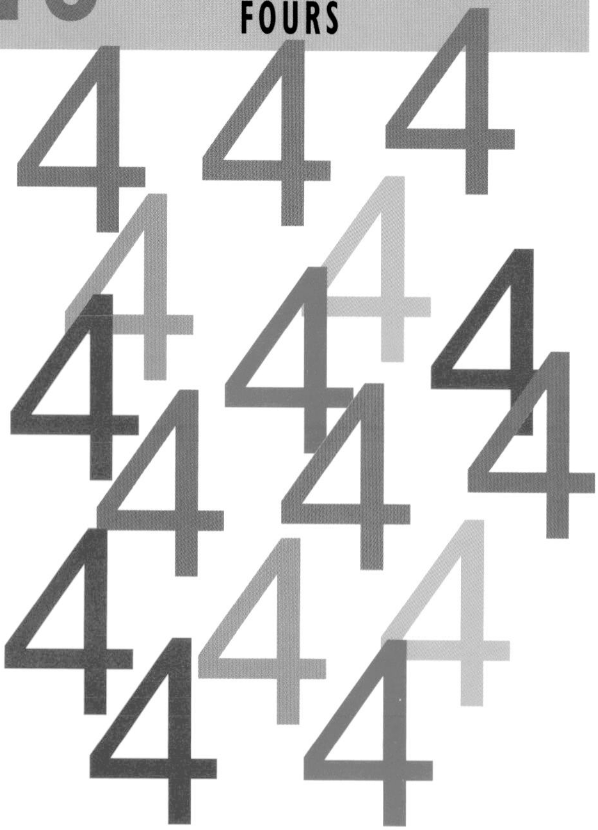

How many fours do you need to reach 500?

11 A DINNER PARTY

Whenever a table arrangement needs to be made up, problems arise. This applies to the occasion shown on the next page as well. To give you an idea: Genevieve has Marc on her right side. Andrea sits next to Frank. But Louise and Genevieve are not sitting next to each other. And the ladies all have pink napkins. So who sits where at this table?

THE BIG BRAIN WORKOUT

1 TRIANGLES
(There is one other solution.)

2 AS HIGH AS POSSIBLE

```
    431
   x52
 22412
```

3 FITTING AND MEASURING

4 DISTURBING STAINS

```
4539281706
        2x
9078563412
```

5 A BIKE RIDE
The distance is 22 kilometers.
Nelly walks 2 kilometers in half an hour.
She has now traveled half the 1.5 hours (so
it is 45 minutes later) it takes her to get to
her mother's house. She then moves at a
speed of 8 km/hour, so that takes her 15
minutes. In those 15 minutes she has traveled 2 kilometers. She has biked at a speed
of 24km/hour so that is 18 km. 2+2+18=22.

6 TRICKY!
19. The number in column one plus
column three is column two plus one.

7 MADE-TO-MEASURE
They are the same length.

8 CHICKEN LOGIC
An egg takes 18 days to get hatched. So it
takes 18 days regardless of the number of
hens, eggs or chicken coops.

9 A ROUND NUMBER

10 FOURS
8 fours
```
    4
    4
    4
   44
 444+
  500
```

11 A DINNER PARTY
Genevieve = 5   Louise = 4
Marc = 6   Frank = 3
John = 1   Andrea = 2

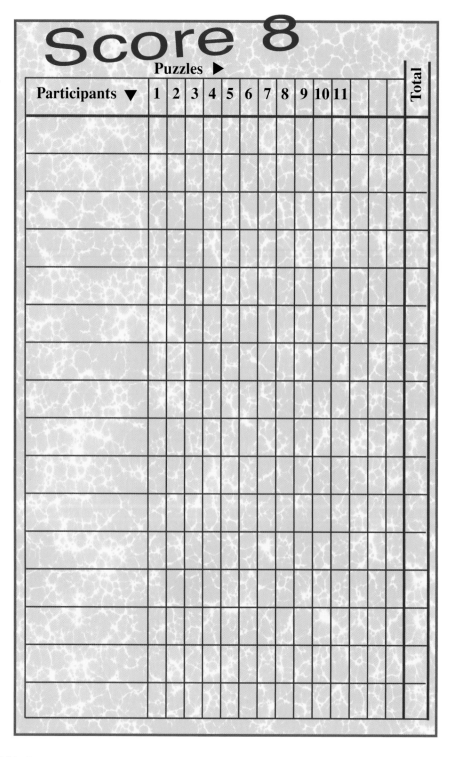
Participants ▼	1	2	3	4	5	6	7	8	9	10	11			Total

Puzzles ▶

SECTION 9

THE BIG BRAIN WORKOUT

1 GRANNIES

Which of these grannies is the tallest? Trace them, cut them out, and change places to compare.

2 SUPER-DUPER DIFFICULT MAGIC SQUARE

1	2	3	4	5	6	7
1	2	3	4	5	6	7
1	2	3	4	5	6	7
1	2	3	4	5	6	7
1	2	3	4	5	6	7
1	2	3	4	5	6	7
1	2	3	4	5	6	7

Cut seven paper strips, write the numbers 1 through 7 and arrange as above. Now, cut through six of the strips once so that, when the pieces are rearranged, also in seven columns of seven numbers, it creates a magic square in which all lines, columns and both diagonals add up to the same total. Very difficult!

3 WAX

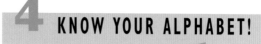

What was wax before wax was wax?

4 KNOW YOUR ALPHABET!

MAN
OAL
LZ?

Which letter should be where the question mark is now?

THE BIG BRAIN WORKOUT

5   LABYRINTH

Find your way from the opening above into the maze
to its center.

6   EGGS

Using three straight lines, divide this group of eggs so
that all the eggs are separated by a line or lines.

7   BURNING ISSUE

Move one match to another place so this equation
corresponds.

8   CLEOPATRA

Was Cleopatra a queen of Egyptian origin?

SECTION 9   **59**

9 FROM 1 THROUGH 8

1	8	7	4
2	3	6	5

Copy the above illustration or trace it. Now fold the whole thing on the dotted lines in such a way that the figures are ordered in the correct sequence, below each other with number 1 first and number 8 last. It doesn't matter if the numbers are upside down or underneath the paper.

10 MARRIAGE?

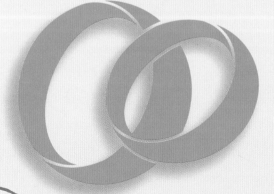

Can a man legally marry the sister of his widow?

THE CHAIN

An "Unending Chain" puzzle, published by Simone Cuny in 1893 in Paris. Your task is to position the pieces into a square, but in such a way that the chain is uninterrupted. Trace the puzzle pieces or copy this page to find the solution.

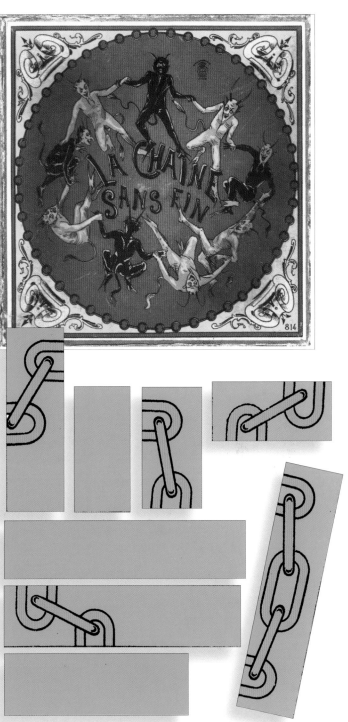

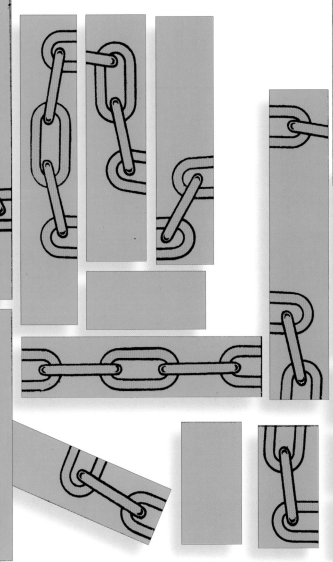

THE BIG BRAIN WORKOUT

1 GRANNIES
Both are the same size.

2 SUPER-DUPER DIFFICULT MAGIC SQUARE

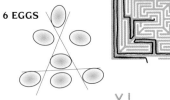

1	2	3	4	5	6	7
3	4	5	6	7	1	2
5	6	7	1	2	3	4
7	1	2	3	4	5	6
2	3	4	5	6	7	1
4	5	6	7	1	2	3
6	7	1	2	3	4	5

3 WAX
Before wax was wax, wax was honey!

4 KNOW YOUR ALPHABET!
The N. The letters represent their position in the alphabet. The first column plus the third is the second. After Z comes A.

5 LABYRINTH

6 EGGS

7 BURNING ISSUE

$$\frac{XL}{VIII} = V$$

8 CLEOPATRA
No, Cleopatra was part of the Ptolemaic dynasty, a Macedonic-Greek line of rulers, and was therefore Greek.

9 FROM 1 THROUGH 8
Rotate the piece of paper so the blank side is toward you and the 2 is in the upper left-hand corner. Then fold the right side against the left so the 5 lies against the 2. Now fold the bottom half upward, so the 4 lies against the 5, then fold the 4 and 5 flap in between the 6 and 3. Finally, fold the 1 and 2 onto the small pile, and it's done.

10 MARRIAGE?
Only dead men have widows, so legality does not even come into the question.

11 THE CHAIN

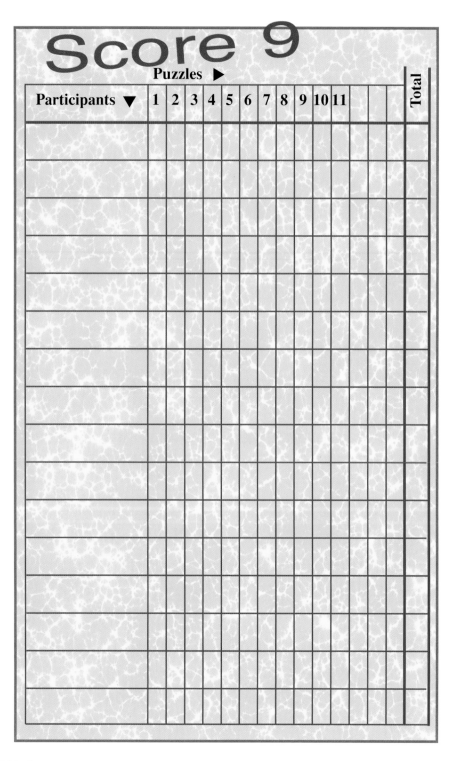

Score 9

Participants ▼	1	2	3	4	5	6	7	8	9	10	11			Total

Puzzles ▶

SECTION 10

THE BIG BRAIN WORKOUT

1 — PROGRESS?

24 10 8 11
16 15 26 13
11 13 10 2
13 22 8

This makes your lives easier and more productive, but when it stops, it causes a lot of irritation. Still almost everybody has learned to deal with it on a daily level, for work or pleasure. What is it?

2 — VAGUE QUESTION MARK

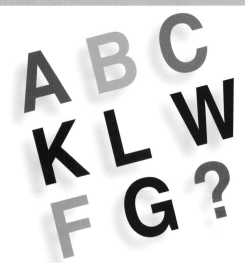

What letter should replace the question mark?

3 — ROLLING AROUND

Put two coins of the same size next to each other on a table. If coin B is turned once all the way around coin A, how many times will coin B revolve around its own center?

4 — TYPICAL TYPEWRITER

Bagart

Bayton

Bekrshyid

Krdnsan

The couples whose names are typed out above used to be very famous on the big screen and sometimes also in love.

5 EXCHANGE RATE PROBLEMS

With the exchange rate rising, this man is obviously happy. Ten minutes later, however, there is a fall in prices and the expression on the man's face changes. Can you find that other expression?

6 BRAIN CRACKER

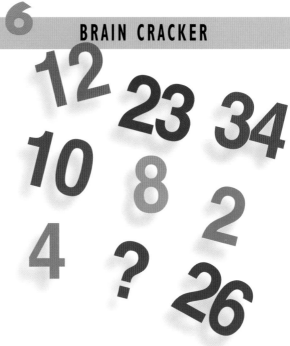

Which number should replace the question mark?

7 A LADYBIRD'S MESS

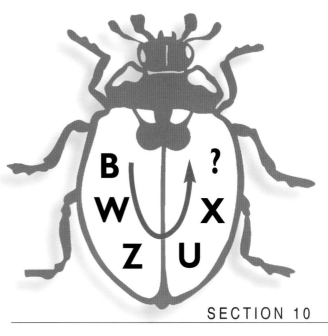

Logically speaking, which letter should replace the question mark?

8 DOODLING 1

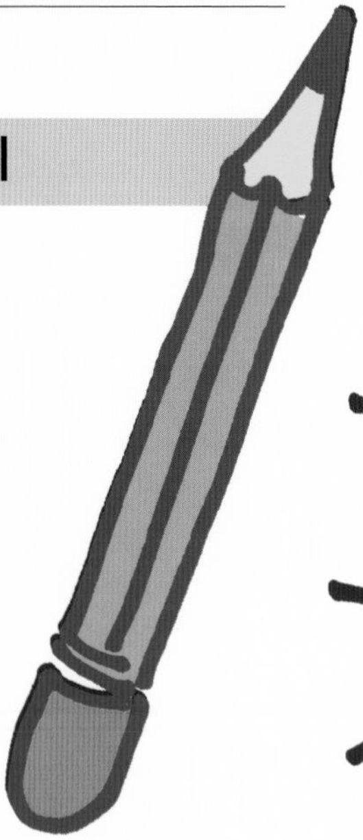

Let's take a moment to doodle. Doodles are quick sketches of images. What do these represent?

1

2

3

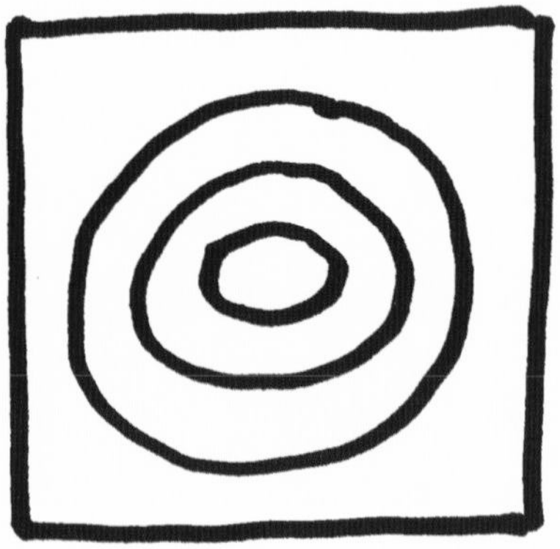

4

5

6

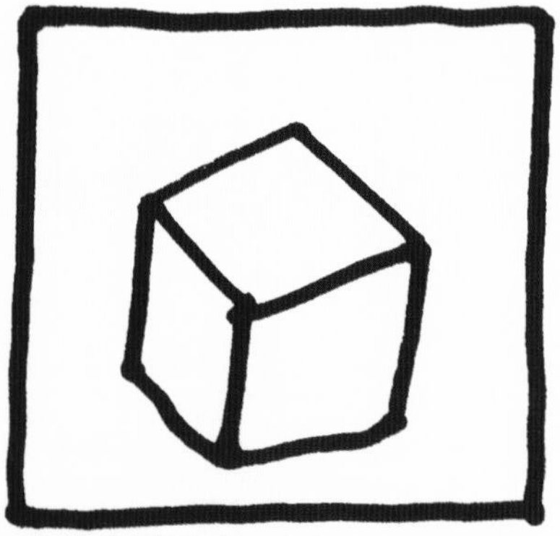

7

8

9 DOVETAILS

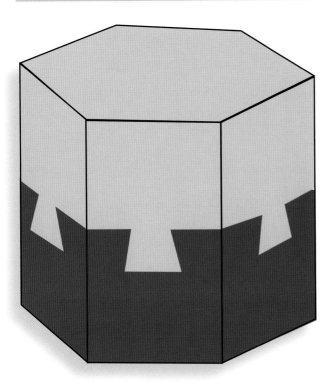

Dovetail joints have been used in the wood business for centuries, and they are still used today for various purposes. But there's something very special about the above construction. How was it put together?

10 APPLES

Read carefully!
If there are five apples and you take three of them.
How many apples do you have now?

THE BIG BRAIN WORKOUT

1 PROGRESS?
Computer program. The numbers represent the position of the letters in the alphabet, less five.

2 VAGUE QUESTION MARK
The M. The letters represent their numerical position in the alphabet. The first column plus the second is the third.

3 ROLLING AROUND
Twice.

4 TYPICAL TYPEWRITER
Bogart – Bacall, Taylor – Burton, Ackroyd – Belushi, Cruise – Kidman

5 EXCHANGE RATE PROBLEMS

6 BRAIN CRACKER
15. In each column, the top row number minus that in the bottom row have 8 as the sum. In the middle row, the first column number minus that in the third column also sums to 8, and 8 is in the center.

7 A LADYBIRD'S MESS
S. The letters represent their numerical position in the alphabet. Thus, based on their position, certain relationships between the letters are created: B-5=W, W+3=Z, Z-5 =U, U+3=X, X-5=S. The repeating elements are −5 and +3.

8 DOODLING
1 A cuttlefish cuddles his wife fondly.
2 Tic-tac-toe played by two very stupid players.
3 A very fat man wearing a cowboy hat, as seen from above.
4 An owl hiding in a crate of oranges.
5 An oyster that has made a mistake.
6 A tired tennis ball.
7 Two times four.
8 A painter's ladder. He's in the hospital.

9 DOVETAILS
In contrast to what a dovetail might lead you to expect, the joints here are diagonal instead of crosswise.

10 APPLES
Then you have three apples!

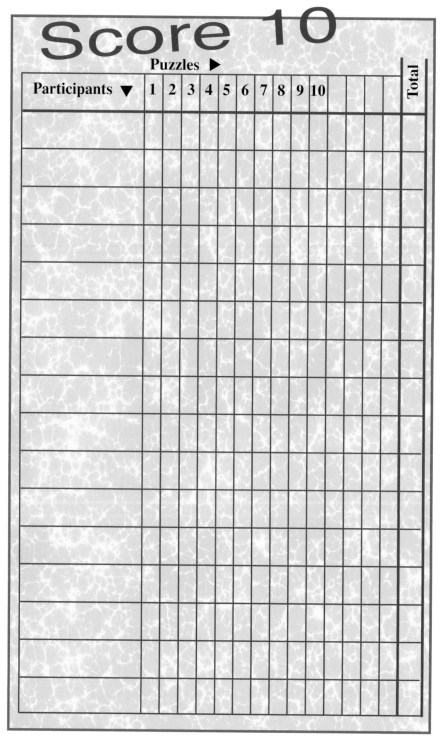

Participants ▼	Puzzles ▶ 1	2	3	4	5	6	7	8	9	10				Total

SECTION II

THE BIG BRAIN WORKOUT

1   RIDDLE WITH COINS

In the cross of coins pictured above, can you move two coins in such a way that each arm of the cross has as many coins as the others do?

2   ANAGRAMS

Ericnhih Ehnie
Helracs Knedics
Sleuj Nerev
Sjeam Cojey
Rhaagm Negere

Can you decipher the names of these world-famous writers from various countries?

3   A GAME OF DOMINOES

You get 18 pips to place on the dominoes pictured here. But it must be done under the following conditions: the total number of pips on the top half must equal the total number of pips on the bottom half. The first domino must have double the number of pips as the fourth. One domino has only one dot and another domino is a "double" one. Furthermore, three dominoes have the same number of dots on their top half, and two others have the same number of dots on their bottom half. It's gonna be a tough day...

4 POSITIONING NUMBERS

Place the numbers 1 through 9 in a triangle, but in such a way that the sum of each side amounts to 17.

5 TRAVELING

Two friends are on the same plane to the U.S. One says to the other: "If I were to give you ten dollars, we would each have the same amount of money. However, if you were to give me ten dollars, I would have twice as much money on me as you would." How much money is each of them carrying?

6 SIMULTANEOUS

Can you simultaneously draw a circle with your left hand and a square with your right hand?

7 EYES AND PAWS

Which animal has eyes on its paws and teeth on its tongue?

THE BIG BRAIN WORKOUT

8   THE QUIZ

When aristocratic gentlemen want to be admitted to a club, they also have to be quizzed. The gentleman pictured here did not know the answer to the question asked. The question was as follows: How do "you boil an egg for two minutes if you only have two egg-timers at your disposal—one of five and one of three minutes—to set the time?

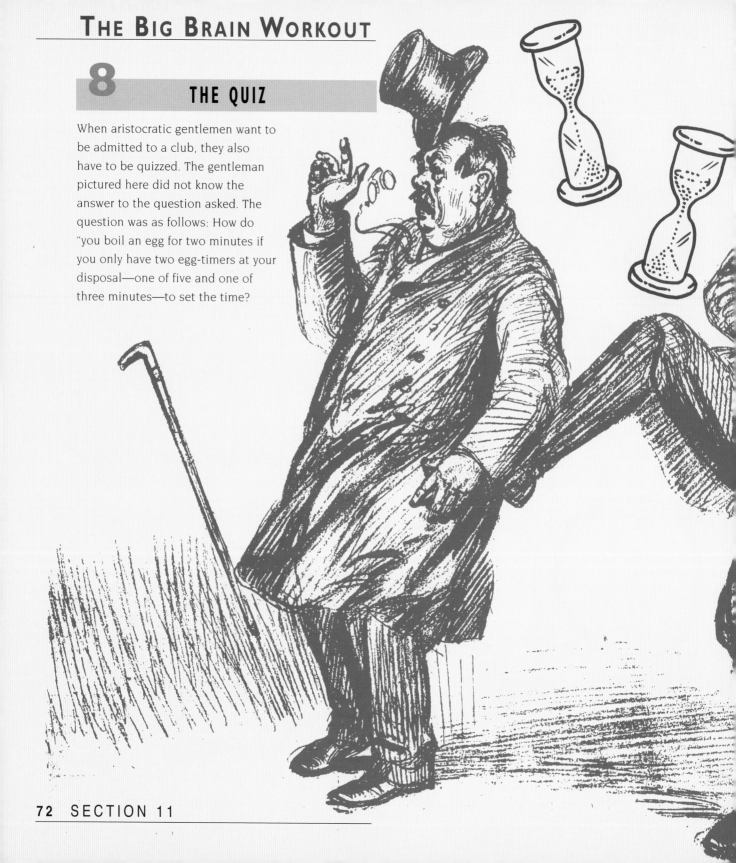

9 35 PENCILS

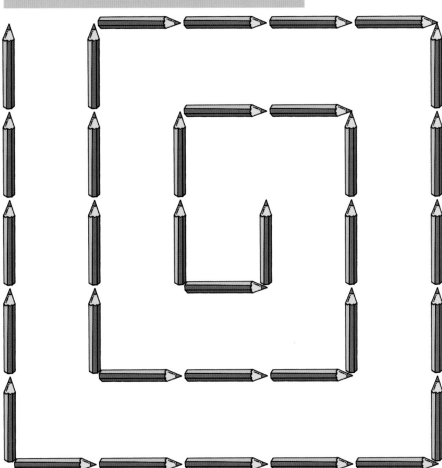

Empty your coloring box and put 35 pencils in a spiral as pictured here. Now move four of the pencils so that you create four perfect squares. If you don't have enough colored pencils at your disposal you can, of course, also work this puzzle using toothpicks or some other suitable objects.

10 THE STOLEN PIPE

Besides their regular products, such as bouillon cubes, the Liebig firm also produced puzzle cards with picture puzzles. The text of this one reads: "Somebody is smoking in here. Where is the pipe?" It is up to you to find it.

THE BIG BRAIN WORKOUT

1 RIDDLE WITH COINS
Take the two coins from the ends of the long arms and position them on top of the middle coin.

2 ANAGRAMS
Heinrich Heine, Charles Dickens, Jules Verne, James Joyce, Graham Greene

3 A GAME OF DOMINOES

4 POSITIONING NUMBERS

5 TRAVELING
One has 70 dollars and the other one 50 dollars.

6 SIMULTANEOUS
It is hard, but possible. If you can do it, mark it on your score sheet.

7 EYES AND PAWS
A snail.

8 THE QUIZ
Turn both egg timers around at the same time. When the 3-minute egg timer is empty, put the egg in boiling water and wait for the 5-minute egg timer to empty. Don't forget to plunge the egg into cold water.

9 35 PENCILS

10 THE STOLEN PIPE

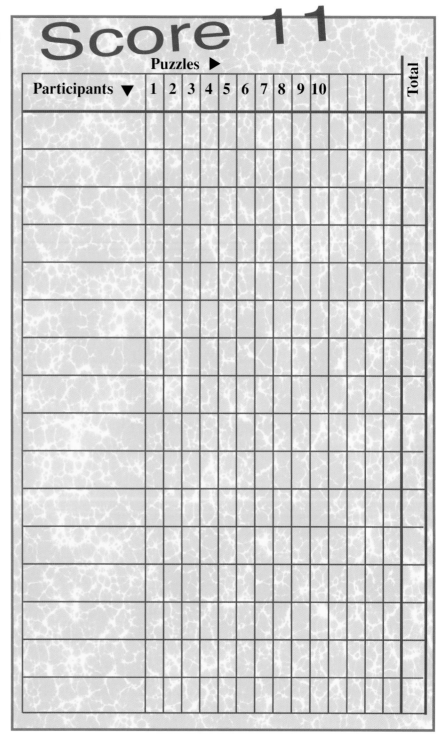

Participants ▼	Puzzles ▶ 1	2	3	4	5	6	7	8	9	10				Total

THE BIG BRAIN WORKOUT

1 INTERNATIONAL CALLING

3645263
667929
77246

Which three European countries are being called here?

2 IN BALANCE

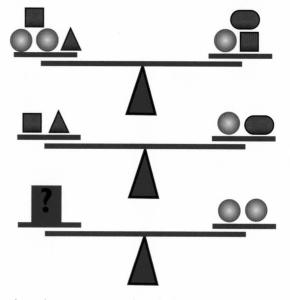

Replace the question mark with the object needed to keep things in balance.

3 MAGIC SQUARE

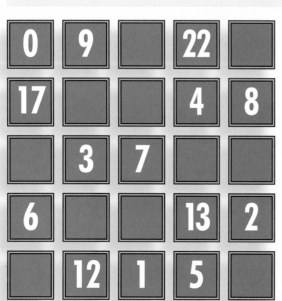

0	9		22	
17			4	8
	3	7		
6			13	2
	12	1	5	

Try to add numbers to the empty boxes in such a way that a magic square is created. A magic square is a square made up of numbers in which all the columns, rows and diagonals add up to the same total. Use the numbers 0 through 24. The magic total is 60.

4 TO THE CENTER

Find your way to the center of the labyrinth.

5 MULTIPLE PERSONALITY

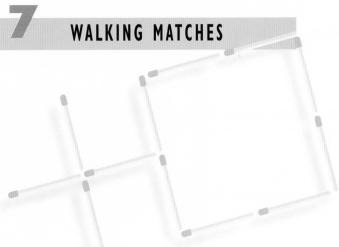

Where is the other personality hidden?

6 SCREWY BOLTS?

If the two similar bolts in the illustration above are screwed in the same direction, do the heads move towards or away from each other?

7 WALKING MATCHES

By moving only five matches, make three squares that are exactly the same.

THE BIG BRAIN WORKOUT

8 STRAIGHT OR BENT?

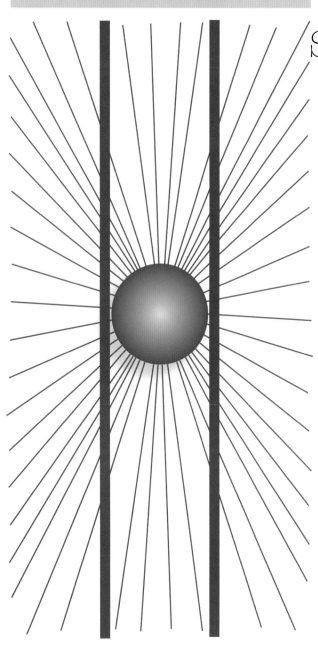

Are the two thick lines in the above drawing straight or do they curve?

9 PECULIAR TYPING

supermarket

spaghetti

oatmeal

sandwich

What words here are typed on top of each other. They all have to do with the kitchen and food shopping.

10 ANNOYING QUESTION MARKS

Which letters belong in place of the question marks?

DOODLING 2

Let's take a moment to doodle. Doodles are quick sketches of all kinds of things. What are these?

THE BIG BRAIN WORKOUT

1 INTERNATIONAL CALLING
England
Norway
Spain

2 IN BALANCE

3 MAGIC SQUARE

4 TO THE CENTER

0	9	18	22	11
17	21	10	4	8
14	3	7	16	20
6	15	24	13	2
23	12	1	5	19

5 MULTIPLE PERSONALITY

6 SCREWY BOLTS?
They stay at the same distance.

7 WALKING MATCHES

8 STRAIGHT OR BENT?
The lines are straight.

9 PECULIAR TYPEWRITER
storekeeper - supermarket
spaghetti - hamburger
lettuce - oatmeal
meatloaf - sandwich

10 ANNOYING QUESTION MARKS
P and F. The letters represent their numerical position in the alphabet. The first column plus the third is the second. The same applies diagonally from top left to bottom right: B+?=H.

DOODLING 2
1 Two kissing snails.
2 Man smoking a really bad cigar.
3 Worm with a bad memory.
4 A 15-Dollar hamburger.
5 Worm on roller skates.
6 What a fly sees the moment before it is crushed dead.
7 Old garage, new car.
8 Two people sharing a tiny seat.
9 Rich sardine in can.

Score 12

Participants ▼	1	2	3	4	5	6	7	8	9	10	11			Total

Puzzles ▶

THE BIG BRAIN WORKOUT

1 GEORGE BUSH SENIOR

Here, George is claiming that he, his son and his grandson together are one hundred years old. According to him, Junior is 24 years younger than his father and 35 years older than his son. What are the ages of these three males?

2 HORSEBACK RIDING

Is this horsewoman moving towards or away from you?

3 WELL-KNOWN WOMEN

38 42 10
14 36 2 12
40 30 28

8 18 2 28
12 30 38 38 50

Who are these two women? One writes mysteries alphabetically; the other's death is an unsolved mystery.

4 UP THERE?

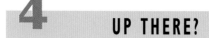
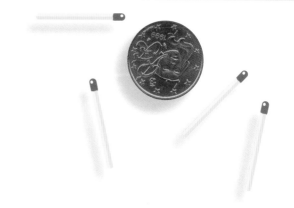

Let's say you present your co-puzzler with the following problem. Take a coin and four matches and ask him or her to put them on the table in such a way that neither the match heads nor the coin touch the table. Do you know the solution?

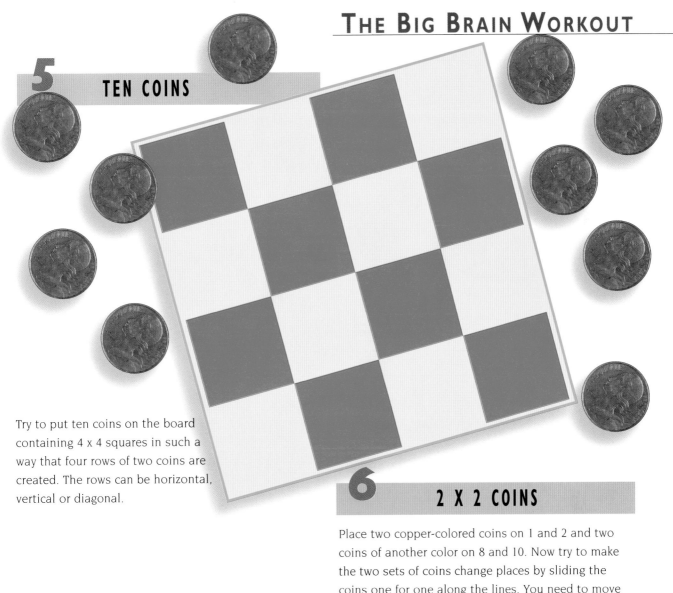

5 TEN COINS

Try to put ten coins on the board containing 4 x 4 squares in such a way that four rows of two coins are created. The rows can be horizontal, vertical or diagonal.

6 2 X 2 COINS

Place two copper-colored coins on 1 and 2 and two coins of another color on 8 and 10. Now try to make the two sets of coins change places by sliding the coins one for one along the lines. You need to move them no more than 18 times. A few rules: no coin may be moved twice in a row, and no coins of different colors may be on the same line.

7 CONTEST

Stan and Oliver, both in top condition, are running 50 yards and back. Stan covers 1.5 yards with every stride and Oliver only one yard. But Oliver is no slouch either: he takes three strides in the time Stan needs to take two. Who wins the competition?

8 NEXT, PLEASE...

What number should replace the question mark above?

9 MODERN-DAY PHENOMENA

byte

string

satellite

computer

Our peculiar typewriter has been at it again. These are all names of modern-day items and phenomena.

10 A LADYBIRD'S MESS

Thinking logically, which letter should replace the question mark?

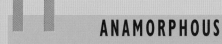

ANAMORPHOUS

Can you make out what this is? We can tell you that
the drawing is over 200 years old; i.e., was made in a
time when the computer did not yet exist. It might
also help to give it some reflection.

1 GEORGE BUSH SENIOR

If all three were the same age, three times the age of Senior would be 100. But Junior is 24 years younger and the grandson is 24+35=59 years younger than Senior. The latter's age can be determined by dividing the total of 100+ 24+59 (=183) by 3. This means Senior is 61 years old, Junior is 37 and the grandson 2 years old. (As you may have guessed, this took place some time ago!

2 HORSEBACK RIDING

Whatever you like; it's a question of how you look at it. Both answers are correct.

3 WELL-KNOWN WOMEN

Sue Grafton, Dian Fosse. The figures represent the position of the letters in the alphabet, multiplied by two.

4 UP THERE?

5 TEN COINS

6 2 X 2 COINS

The moves are: 2-3, 8-5, 10-7, 3-9, 5-2, 7-4, 9-6, 4-10, 6-8, 1-6, 2-4, 6-5, 4-3, 10-9, 5-7, 3-2, 9-1, and 7-10.

7 CONTEST

Oliver wins. He has to take exactly 100 strides to cover the distance back and forth. Stan, however, has to take 33 steps to cover 49.5 meters, which means he has to take an additional stride to cross the turning point and ends up a yard short. Thus, Stan has to take 38 steps to cover the whole distance. He only walks two-thirds faster than Oliver—so in the time Oliver takes 100 steps, Stan only takes 66.66 steps, i.e. 99.99 yards.

8 NEXT, PLEASE...

16. In this sequence, numbers are doubled in turns.

9 MODERN-DAY PHENOMENA

file - byte
stress - jetlag
cellphone - satellite
computer - internet

10 A LADYBIRD'S MESS

N. The letters represent their position in the alphabet. On that basis, certain letter relationships are created: Dx2=8=H, H-3=5=E, Ex2=10=J, J-3=7=G, Gx2=14=N. The repeating elements are x2 and −3.

11 ANAMORPHOUS

Put a reflecting cylinder on the spot in the middle to see the result.

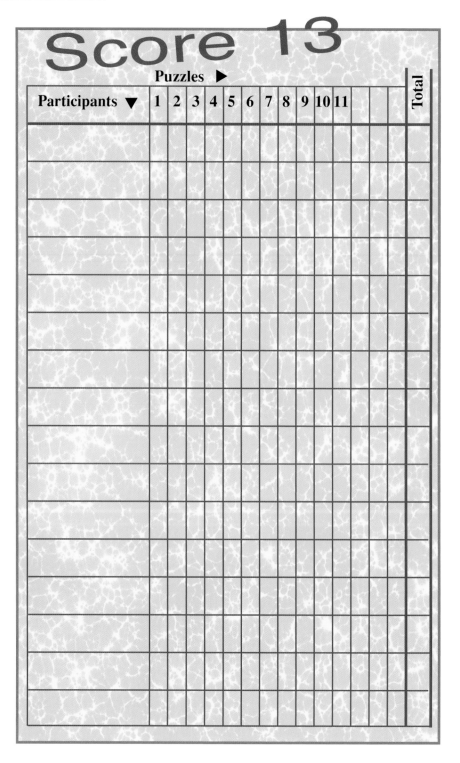

Participants ▼	Puzzles ▶											Total
	1	2	3	4	5	6	7	8	9	10	11	

Score 13

SECTION 14

1 QUITE A TIE

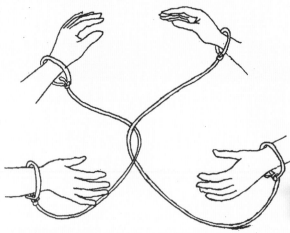

Use two pieces of string to tie you and a friend together as shown above. Now, try to free yourself from the strings without untying the knots.

2 ANAGRAMS

Teneimt Traswel
Hurt Ldenler
Tgahaa Trecihis
Ticpiraa Nelcrowl
Cicni Cnrefh

Crime pays for these authors. All have crime to thank for their fame.

3 TRAINS

Every ten minutes, a train leaves from a city's central station to a station in a suburb. The ride takes 45 minutes. The driver of the train takes a five-minute break before departure and after arrival, in the city as well as in the suburb. How many trains per hour are there on this route?

4 INTERNATIONAL CALLING

793336
2354486
76788425

Which European countries are being called here?

5 CHESS-DOMINO

Can you lay 31 dominoes on a chessboard to cover each square once? The only exceptions are the A1 (top left) square and H8 (bottom right) squares, which are to remain empty.

6 IN BETWEEN THE WAISTS

An American advertisement from 1890. The idea is to put the corset on the lady without cutting, bending or tearing the card (or this page). Can you manage?

7 EVERY MAN TO HIS TRADE

The cobbler's wife keeps an eye on her husband to make sure he is working. Where is she?

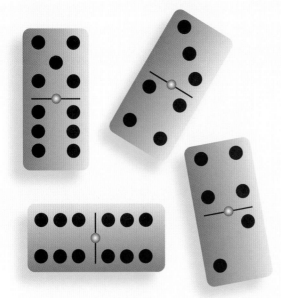

8 PASTA MAZE

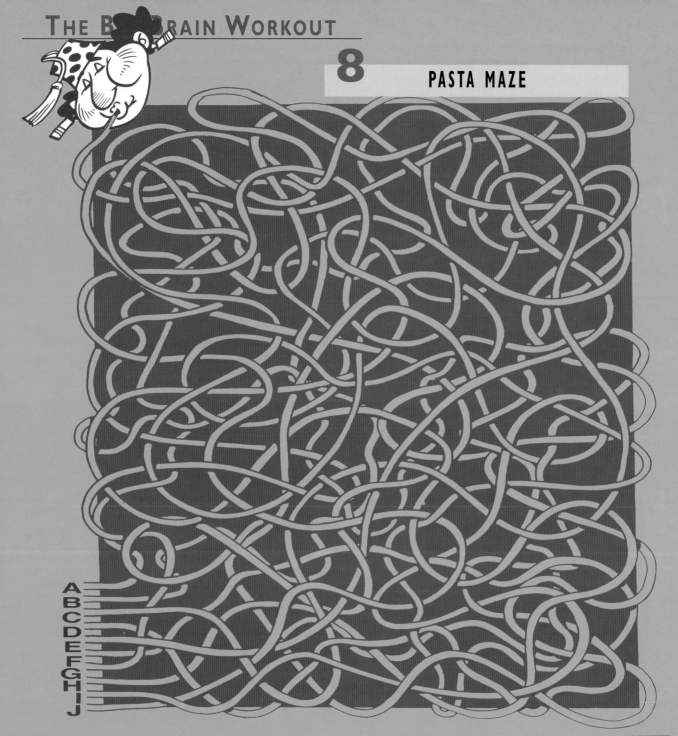

A
B
C
D
E
F
G
H
I
J

Which strand of spaghetti is connected to the eater above? Try and solve this puzzle visually; that is, without using a pencil or anything like that.

9 KNIGHT ON A HORSE

To solve this problem you don't need to be a chess player but you do have to be familiar with the moves of a knight on the chessboard: Two squares forward in any direction and one square to the left or the right of the move. 16 pieces have been placed on the chessboard. Your task is to remove these pieces from the board in 17 successive moves.

THE BIG BRAIN WORKOUT

1 QUITE A TIE
Take a loop and thrust it through the loop around the wrist of the other. Pull the loop around the hand and pull the whole thing loose.

2 ANAGRAMS
Minette Walters
Ruth Rendell
Agatha Christie
Patricia Cornwell
Nicci French

3 TRAINS
There is a train every 10 minutes. This means there are five trains en route at the moment that train 1 arrives at the suburban station. Train 1 waits five minutes, so it is 50 minutes later when it leaves to go back to the city station. At the same moment train 6 leaves that station. This means that by the time train 1 arrives at central station there are ten trains en route.

4 INTERNATIONAL CALLING
Sweden, Belgium, Portugal

5 CHESS-DOMINO
It is not possible. Due to the fact that two squares remain empty, the board has 32 white and 30 black squares left. If you put 30 dominoes on the board there will be two white squares left and you can never cover them with one piece, because they are not next to each other.

6 IN BETWEEN THE WAISTS
Bring the page closer to your eyes while you keep looking at the green line in the middle. The corset will make its way to the lady.

7 EVERY MAN TO HIS TRADE

8 PASTA MAZE
Strand F

9 KNIGHT ON A HORSE
The first move can be made with any piece except C4, D3, D4, E5, E6 and F5. If you start with the knight on A3 with C2 as first piece to capture, then de pieces B4, D3, B2, C4, D2, B3, D4, E6, G7, F5, E7, G6, E5, F7 and G5 follow.

Score 14

Participants ▼	Puzzles ▶ 1	2	3	4	5	6	7	8	9				Total

SECTION 15

THE BIG BRAIN WORKOUT

1   25 LITTLE BALLS

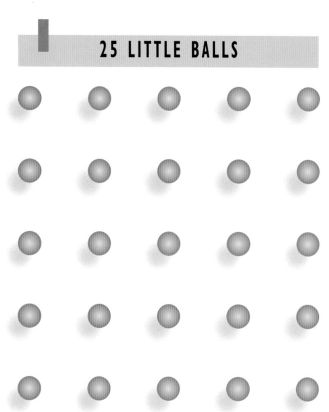

Connect twelve of these little balls by straight lines so that a perfect cross is created, with five balls inside and eight balls outside the cross.

2   MAGIC SQUARE

11	24		20	3
4		25		16
	5	13	21	
10		1		22
23	6		2	15

This magic square has 65 as the magic total. The only problem is, some of the numbers are missing. Can you correct this situation? All the numbers from 1 through 25 can be used, but only once.

3   BACK TO SCHOOL?

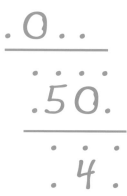

A six-digit number is divided by a three-digit number. The result is also a three-digit number. Which numbers are we talking about here?

4   WHAT'S WRONG?

Something's just not right in this picture. What is it?

5 BIZARRE LETTERS

What letter should replace the question mark?

6 DOVETAIL 2

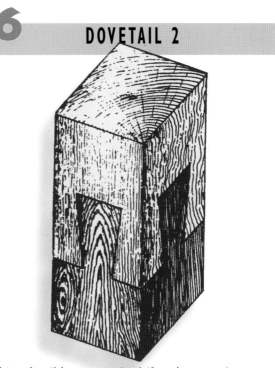

Is this a feasible construcion? If so, how was it put together?

7 YEARS THAT COUNT

John is 24 years old; twice as old as Mary was when John was just as old as Mary is now. How old is Mary?

8 CAPITAL

CNGWBGPGX

What do we have here? Who changed the letters around in the typewriter? And then also garbled the name? It concerns a South American country.

9 MISCHIEVOUS MATCHES

Try to create a figure of four squares by moving seven of these matches.

10 WITCHES' PUZZLE

Here is an advertisement puzzle, dating from 1938, for Dickinson's Witch Hazel, a shaving astringent. The idea here is to get the witches to sit on the backs of the cats without folding or cutting the three cards. Trace the cards and give it a try.

11 LION'S SHARE

Look real close. Can you find six former British colonies?

12 HALF AN EGG IS NOT AN EGG

A woman at the market sold half of her supply of eggs plus half an egg to Mr. Johnson. Then she sold half of the rest of her supply plus half an egg to Mr. Smith. Subsequently, Mr. Koch bought half of the rest of her supply plus half an egg. And then Mr. Kohl bought the remainding 33. How many eggs did the market woman have when she started out? And by the way, she did not sell any broken eggs.

1 25 LITTLE BALLS

2 MAGIC SQUARE

11	24	7	20	3
4	12	25	8	16
17	5	13	21	9
10	18	1	14	22
23	6	19	2	15

3 BACK TO SCHOOL?

123195:215=573

4 WHAT'S WRONG?

A polar bear in a tropical setting

5 BIZARRE LETTERS

W. The letters represent their numerical position in the alphabet. The top row plus the bottom one is the middle one in each column. After Z, continue counting through the A.

6 DOVETAIL 2

7 YEARS THAT COUNT

Mary is 18 years old.

8 CAPITAL

Venezuela (the position in the alphabet plus two, written back to front).

9 MISCHIEVOUS MATCHES

10 WITCHES' PUZZLE

11 LION'S SHARE

They are written in the lion's mane:
Canada
India
Australia
New Zealand
African Colonies

12 HALF AN EGG IS NOT AN EGG

271 eggs. Johnson bought 135.5+0.5= 136 eggs, so there were 135 eggs left. Smith bought 67.5+0.5=68 eggs, so there were 67 eggs left. Koch bought 33.5+0.5 =34 eggs, so 33 eggs remained, and they were bought by Kohl.

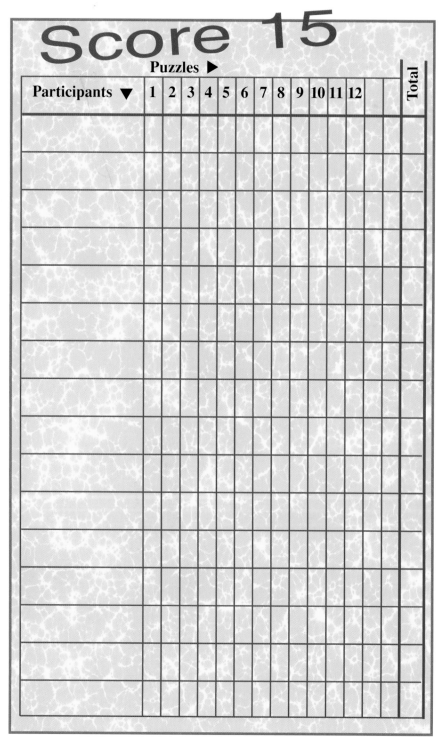

Participants ▼	1	2	3	4	5	6	7	8	9	10	11	12	Total

Score 15
Puzzles ▶

SECTION 16

THE BIG BRAIN WORKOUT

1 WHAT'S WRONG?

What is wrong in this drawing?

2 ANAGRAM ANOTHER WAY

CDFGHKMN PQRTVWXYZ

Above are letters you do not need for this anagram. The other letters of the alphabet, which you do need, form the name of a wine region in France. Note: One vowel is used twice.

3 FITTING AND MEASURING

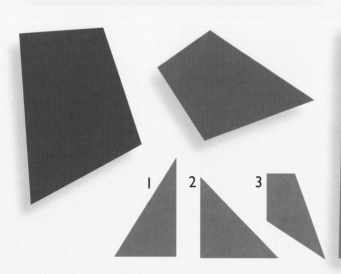

Together, the colored forms shown here would make up a square, that is if one piece weren't missing. Which of the gray figures completes the square?

4 STORM

This ship appears to be on the point of capsizing. Where is the captain?

5 DOUBLE

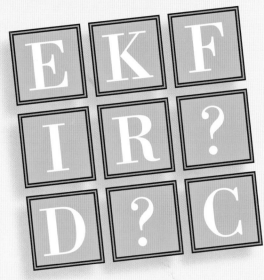

What letters should replace the question marks?

6 GEOMETRY

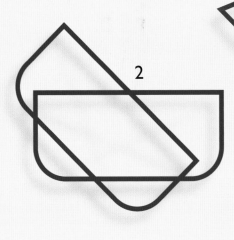

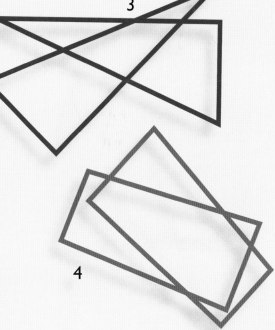

Which of these four figures does not belong?

A	A	B	B	C	C	C	C	D	D	D	A	A	B	B	C
C	C	D	D	D	A	A	B	B	C	C	C	C	D	D	D
A	B	B	C	C	C	C	D	D	D	A	A	B	B	C	C
C	D	D	D	A	A	B	B	C	C	C	C	D	D	D	A
B	B	C	C	C	C	D	D	D	A	A	B	B	C	C	C
D	D	D	A	A	B	B	C	C	C	C	D	D	D	A	A
B	C	C	C	C	D	D	D	A	A	B	B	C	C	C	C
D	D	A	A	B	B	C	C	C				D	A	A	B
C	C	C	C	D	D	D	A	A				C	C	C	D
D	A	A	B	B	C	C	C	C				A	A	B	B
C	C	C	D	D	D	A	A	B	B	C	C	C	C	D	D
A	A	B	B	C	C	C	C	D	D	D	A	A	B	B	C
C	C	D	D	D	A	A	B	B	C	C	C	C	D	D	D
A	B	B	C	C	C	C	D	D	D	A	A	B	B	C	C
C	D	D	D	A	A	B	B	C	C	C	C	D	D	D	A

7 WHICH ONE FITS?

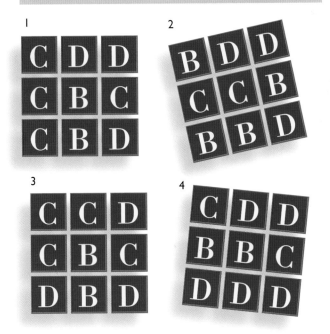

1

C	D	D
C	B	C
C	B	D

2

B	D	D
C	C	B
B	B	D

3

C	C	D
C	B	C
D	B	D

4

C	D	D
B	B	C
D	D	D

Which of the four squares above fits into the hole on the opposite page? It's a question of reading, and reading again...

8 THE ODD COUPLE?

16 18 21 23 12

6 12 4 4 17 7

10 18 16 8 3

4 7 7 4 16 22

On first meeting, they may seem more than a bit strange. But no one can deny that are a very loving couple. What duo are we talking about?

9 SQUARISH PROBLEM

Which number belongs in the bottom right corner of the last square?

12 — 54 — 4
6 — — 5

3 — 66 — 18
6 — — 6

12 — 60 — 9
5 — — 4

24 — 98 — 12
9 — — ?

1 WHAT'S WRONG?
Sails set when yacht is at anchor.

2 ANAGRAM ANOTHER WAY
A B E I J L O S U
Beaujolais

3 FITTING AND MEASURING
No. I

4 STORM

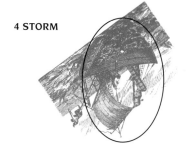

5 DOUBLE
The I (middle right) and the G (middle bottom). The letters represent their numerical position in the alphabet. The letter from the first column plus that of the third column is the letter in the middle column. It works that way horizontally as well as vertically.

6 GEOMETRY
No. 4. The other forms consist of two similar halves of one complete shape.

7 WHICH ONE FITS?
No. 4. The letter sequence from left to right is 2xA, 2xB, 4xC, 3xD, etc.

8 THE ODD COUPLE?
Morticia and Gomez Addams. The numbers represent the position of the letters in the alphabet, but three letters further on.

9 SQUARISH PROBLEM
4. The sum of the corner numbers multiplied by two is the number in the middle.

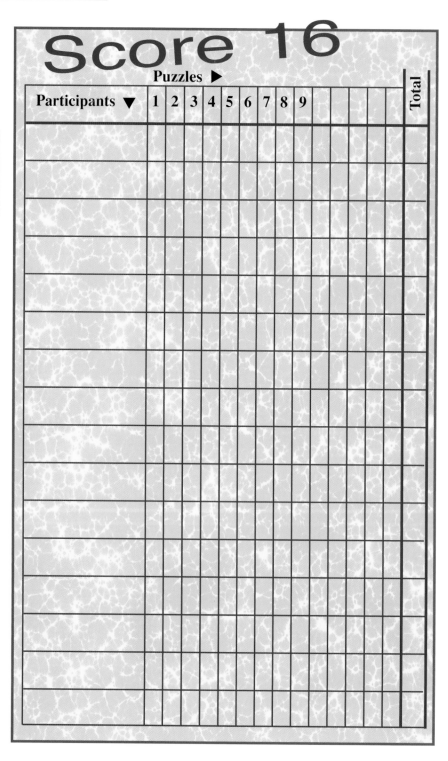

Score 16

Puzzles ▶

Participants ▼	1	2	3	4	5	6	7	8	9				Total

Section 17

THE BIG BRAIN WORKOUT

1 WEIGHTY PROBLEM

In your business you regularly need to weigh packages for shipment. You have found that the packages always weigh between 1 and 40 lbs. You have only one scale and four weights at your disposal. Which four would you pick from the series of weights below?

1, 2, 3, 4, 5, 9, 10, 12, 15, 20, 27, 30 lbs.

2 KNIGHT'S MOVE

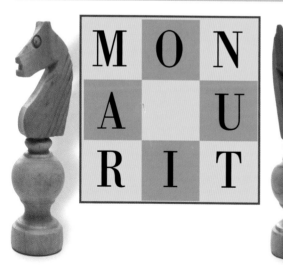

M	O	N
A		U
R	I	T

These letters form a nine-letter word. What is it? Find it by using a knight's moves through the square. The first and last letters of the word are the same.

3 LUNCH

Three ladies—each accompanied by two daughters—want to have lunch in a restaurant. Even though there are only seven chairs available, there is enough space for everyone. How is this possible?

4 TEA TIME

A tea advertisement from 1890, France. Which of these three Chinese is the shortest? Venture a guess before you resort to measuring!

5 A FRESH EGG

A gentleman farmer living on his farm eats two fresh eggs a day. He does not own any chickens. He does not buy or steal his eggs, is not given them and does not get them in exchange for something else. He does not find them and yet he has two nice fresh eggs for breakfast every day. Where do the eggs come from?

6 HERBS & SPICES EXPRESS

сшттфьщт
зуззук
кщыуьфкн
сдщму
сгьшт
зфкыдун
ифышд
сфнутту
ерньу
фтшыу

A warehouse is filled with herbs and spices ready for export. The labels have already been printed albeit, unfortunately, in a kind of Russian. Can you figure out the names? (Hint: y=E)

THE BIG BRAIN WORKOUT

7 BIKE TRIP

This is Henry, after his weekly bike trip to visit his family. Taking it easy, he cycled at a speed of 12 miles per hour, until he got a flat. The next two miles Henry went on foot, and this took half an hour. Then he got a lift from a horse-drawn carriage. He managed to cover the remaining distance to his destination at a speed of eight miles per hour. It took him 1.5 hours to reach the home of his family. Can you figure out the distance?

8 STUNT

Take the lid off of a matchbox and put it on top of the box, as shown above. Now, reverse their order on the table by only touching the lid. Take a deep breath before you start this puzzle!

9 ZOO

Hans has only one hobby: animals. He has fish, birds, mice and cats at his home. His animal collection boasts 15 heads and six wings, plus the patter of 38 little feet. How many fish does Hans have?

10 BELLS

Around Christmas, you normally hear lots of bells ringing. The labyrinth on the opposite page reflects such a situation. In what sequence should the cords be pulled in order to find the word BELL? Don't forget you can pull the same cord twice for the L.

A B C D

THE BIG BRAIN WORKOUT

1 WEIGHTY PROBLEM
1, 3, 9 and 27. You can weigh all the packages from 1 to 40 pounds with these four weights.

2 KNIGHT'S MOVE
Ruminator.

3 LUNCH
A grandmother with her two daughters who each have two daughters. Seven females in total!

4 TEA TIME
All three are the same height.

5 A FRESH EGG
From the farm's goose.

6 HERBS & SPICES EXPRESS
Cinnamon, pepper, rosemary, clove, cumin, parsley, basil, cayenne, thyme, anise.

7 BIKE TRIP
The distance is 12 miles. On foot, two miles takes him half an hour. So there's an hour left. Of this, he covers the other half at a distance of 12 mph—i.e., six miles. The second half and the last half an hour, he moves at 8 mph, thus four miles. 2+6+4=12.

8 STUNT
Suck up the box through the lid, throwing your head back. Then hold the lid with your thumb and forefinger to put the whole thing back on the table.

9 ZOO
6 wings means that Hans has 3 birds – 3 heads and 6 feet. Without the birds, the "zoo" consists of 12 heads and 32 feet. Mice and cats have four each. 32 divided by 4 means 8 cats and mice. Fish have no feet. 12 heads minus 8 means 4 heads, so 4 are fish.

10 BELLS
The combinations are: CDAB, CDBA, CDBB, CDAA.

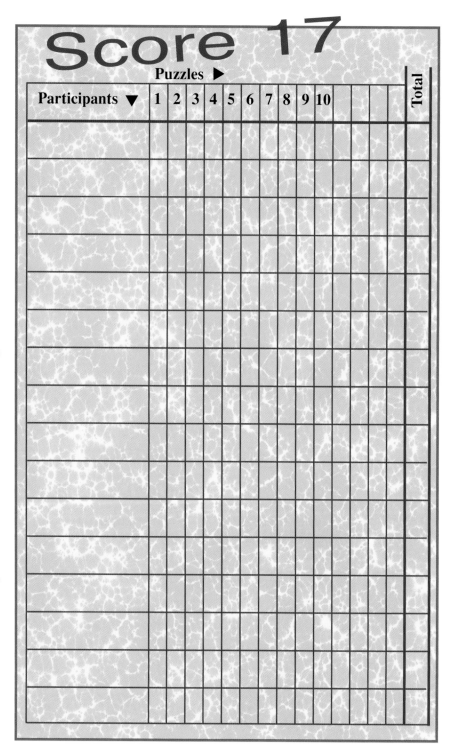

Participants ▼	1	2	3	4	5	6	7	8	9	10					Total

Score 17

Puzzles ▶

THE BIG BRAIN WORKOUT

1 SIX MATCHES

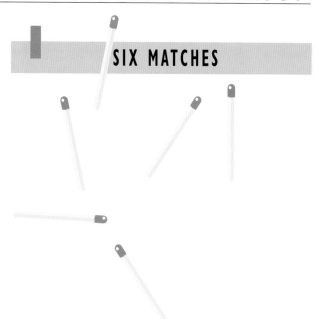

With six matches, make four equilateral triangles.

3 LETTER PROBLEM

Can you find the letter that should go in the box with the question mark?

2 TRIP

Anne-Marie went on a trip through Europe. She thought London was a nice city, but did not care for Amsterdam. She felt Madrid was impressive, but did not like Barcelona. She loved Budapest. In Italy, she adored Rome but found Padua uninteresting. What did she think of Brussels?

4 THERE'S A NIP IN THE AIR

361   441   256   25

324   4   225   529   144

There's a lot of speculation about this yearly sports event. Which event are we talking about?

5 SHOWING THE FLAG

What is the message this sailor is sending to his loved one? A postcard from America, 1908.

6 HIDE AND SEEK

In this American advertisement (1880) for a wringer, a few other things are hidden. Can you find them?
To really get an in-depth look at the problem, try holding it up. It might help to see it in a different light.

7 JUMBLE

Whatever does this mean? Can you make out what is written here to the right?

THE BIG BRAIN WORKOUT

6 HIDE AND SEEK

8 BROTHERLY NUMBERS

107 114
222 510
402 600

Which of these numbers does not belong with the others?

9 THE DEER'S EAR

Find the hare.

10 DOGGERY

How many seconds do 8 dogs need to eat 56 biscuits if each dog needs 5 seconds for one biscuit?

NOSING AROUND

How many noses can you find in this drawing?
A nose is only a nose if it is on a face with eyes,
a mouth and perhaps ears.

THE BIG BRAIN WORKOUT

1 SIX MATCHES

2 TRIP
She liked Brussels. She did not like the cities with the letter A twice in their name.

3 LETTER PROBLEM
E. The letters are in alphabetical order, but two letters are skipped each time. The order is from top left to right, down, to the left, up to the second row, to the right and so on in a spiral.

4 THERE'S A NIP IN THE AIR
The Superbowl. Extract the root of the numbers and the result represents the numerical position of the letter in the alphabet.

5 SHOWING THE FLAG
Sweetheart.

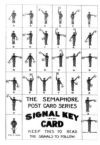

6 HIDE AND SEEK
Hold the page up against light and look through it.

7 JUMBLE
Look diagonally across the "design" from all sides to see "What does this mean."

8 BROTHERLY NUMBERS
107. The other numbers can be divided by 2 and per number add up to 6.

9 THE DEER'S EAR

10 DOGGERY
35 seconds.

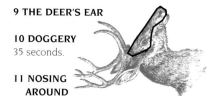

11 NOSING AROUND
15 noses.

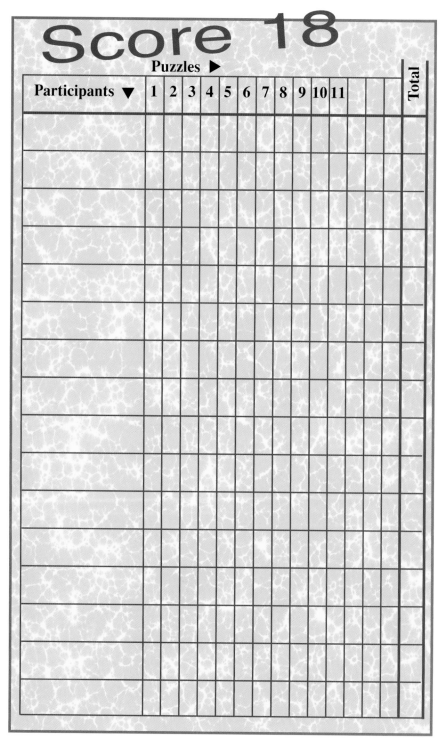

Score 18

Participants ▼	Puzzles ▶ 1	2	3	4	5	6	7	8	9	10	11	Total

SECTION 19

THE BIG BRAIN WORKOUT

1 SIX SHOOTER

The target has six rings with the values 16, 17, 23, 26, 39 and 40. If you want to score 100 with only five shots, which combination of rings do you need to hit?

2 LOGIC?

6 3 1 ?
2 3 ? 2
2 4 3 5
4 2 5 1

What is the logic of this square and, based on that logic, which numbers replace the questions mark?

3 RELATIONSHIPS

The father-in-law of Suzy's husband is the brother-in-law of the brother of Suzy's husband. How are these people related?

4 ANAGRAM?

A B C F G I J
K L M P O Q
S T U V W X Y Z

Above are the letters you do not need. Find the letters you do need and put them in the correct order to form the name of a shrub that has beautiful flowers.
Two of the letters are used twice and two others even three times!

5 CROSS PUZZLE

It is possible to divide the above cross into four parts by making two straight cuts, so that the four parts can form a square. Can you do it?

6 MATCHES

By moving just three matches, change this shape into a cube consisting of three diamonds.

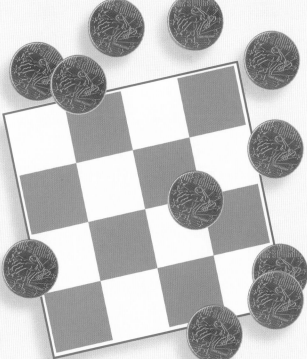

7 SIXTEEN SQUARES

Place eleven coins on the board with the 16 squares pictured here, but do it in a way that creates as many rows of two coins as possible.

8 A MAGIC SQUARE

With four moves you can reorganize these numbers in such a way that they form a magic square. That is to say, the rows with numbers, indicated here by red lines—horizontally, vertically and diagonally—should add up to 15.

9 AN UNUSUAL SERIES

These numbers form a series. In other words, there is a relationship between them. What is this relationship and what number should follow?

10 AGE

Esther is twice as old as Paul was when Esther was as old as Paul is now – 18. How old is Esther?

TURKEY LABYRINTH

Starting at number 4 in the center, take four steps in any direction you wish—horizontally, vertically, or diagonally. Once you arrive at a numbered square, take the number of steps indicated in the square, again in any desired direction. This is how you find your way to the outside of this labyrinth. Your last move, however, should take you exactly one step outside the labyrinth.

Your task is to find your way out of the maze in only three moves.

THE BIG BRAIN WORKOUT

1 SIX SHOOTER
17, 17, 17, 23, 26.

2 LOGIC?

6	3	1	4	14
2	3	5	2	12
2	4	3	5	14
4	2	5	1	12

14 12 14 12

3 RELATIONSHIPS
Suzy's father is married to the sister of Suzy's husband.

4 ANAGRAM?
D E H N O R
Rhododendron.

5 CROSS PUZZLE

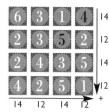

6 MATCHES

7 SIXTEEN SQUARES
You can make 14 rows of two.

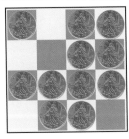

8 A MAGIC SQUARE
1 goes between 8 and 6, 9 between 4 and 2, 7 between 2 and 6, 3 between 4 and 8.

9 AN UNUSUAL SERIES
Each number represents two multiplying factors. 7x7=49, 4x9=36, 3x6=18, 1x8=8, so the next number should be 8.

10 AGE
Esther is 24.

11 TURKEY LABYRINTH
Direction east till 3, southeast till 3 and southward till outside the maze.

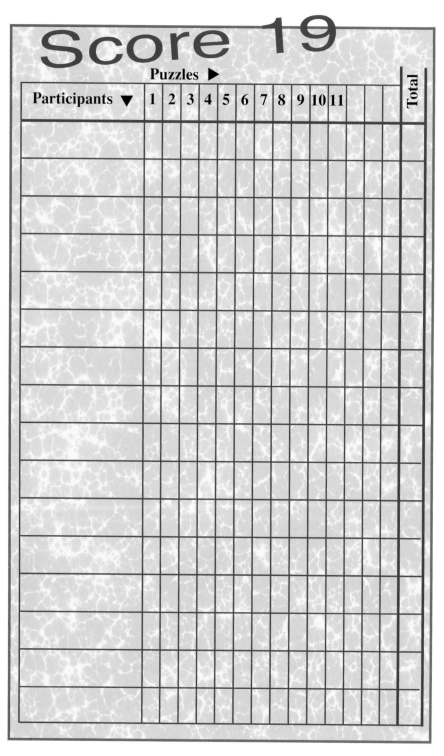

Score 19

Participants ▼	Puzzles ▶ 1	2	3	4	5	6	7	8	9	10	11			Total

PUZZLE COMPETITION
FINALS

Final Scores

▼Participants	Section results ▶																			Total
	1	2	3	4	5	6	7	8	9	10	11	12	13	14	15	16	17	18	19	

I AM THE
SMARTEST

SHOO FLY!

In 1880, a special series of picture puzzles was published. There were only six of them, but the number of hidden persons, animals and objects was enormous. In some of the pictures no less than 164 illustrations were hidden. One of these is shown on the following pages. Its name was "Shoo fly!" Why? See for yourself. The fly was found very quickly. But then there were: a fairy, a peacock, a shark, a butterfly, a lion, a rabbit, a book, a coat, a boot, a hare, a rake, a vat, a dove, an abacus, a caterpillar, a snail, a match, a turtle, an owl, a rhinoceros, an antelope, a clock, a skull, a cat, a cow, a giraffe, a priest, a mummy, a squirrel, five fish, two Indians, Tom Thumb, twelve faces, three mice, eleven dogs, three eagles, five letters without envelopes, five ducks, two camels, three elephants, seven men, two monkeys, two bowls, four birds, four bears, four goats, eight frogs, two seals, three beavers, nine sheep, three ladies, five horses, five pigs, two chickens, four crocodiles, two boys, two babies and two combs!

We'll leave the finding of this solution to you—after all, you've had a good bit of practice by now, and have no doubt acquired a ton of practical experience to help you. So, have fun!

Write down the scores per puzzle section on the page opposite. The person with the highest score is awarded the rosette pictured above. (There's another smaller one on the last page for the person with the lowest score.)

Solutions for the Tangram puzzles on the opening pages of the sections.